A-LEVEL

STUDENT GUIDE

EDEXCEL

Geography

Health, human rights and intervention
Migration, identity and sovereignty

Cameron Dunn

HODDER
EDUCATION
AN HACHETTE UK COMPANY

Hodder Education, an Hachette UK company, Blenheim Court, George Street, Banbury, Oxfordshire OX16 5BH

Orders

Bookpoint Ltd, 130 Park Drive, Milton Park, Abingdon, Oxfordshire OX14 4SB

tel: 01235 827827

fax: 01235 400401

e-mail: education@bookpoint.co.uk

Lines are open 9.00 a.m.–5.00 p.m., Monday to Saturday, with a 24-hour message answering service. You can also order through the Hodder Education website: www.hoddereducation.co.uk

First printed 2019

Impression number 5 4 3 2 1

Year 2023 2022 2021 2020 2019

Cover photo: Kevin Eaves/Fotolia

Typeset by Integra Software Services Pvt Ltd, Pondicherry, India

Printed by Bell & Bain Ltd, Glasgow

Hachette UK's policy is to use papers that are natural, renewable and recyclable products and made from wood grown in well-managed forests and other controlled sources. The logging and manufacturing processes are expected to conform to the environmental regulations of the country of origin.

Contents

■ Getting the most from this book

Exam-style questions

Sample student answers

Practise the questions, then look at the student answers that follow.

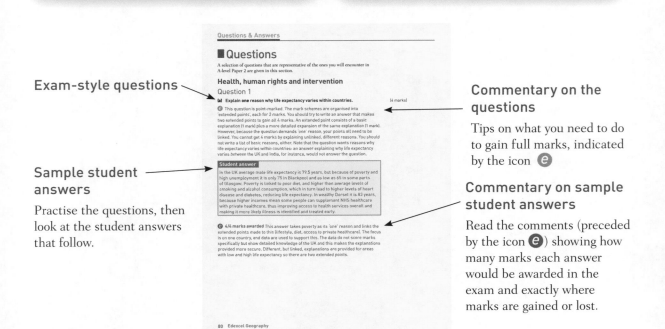

Commentary on the questions

Tips on what you need to do to gain full marks, indicated by the icon **e**

Commentary on sample student answers

Read the comments (preceded by the icon **e**) showing how many marks each answer would be awarded in the exam and exactly where marks are gained or lost.

■About this book

This guide offers advice for the effective revision of the two optional content areas: Option 8A: Health, human rights and intervention and Option 8B: Migration, identity and sovereignty.

The optional content areas are tested in A-level Paper 2. The whole exam (including the other areas of study not covered here) lasts 2 hours and 15 minutes and makes up 30% of the A-level qualification. More information on the external exam papers is given in the Questions & Answers section at the back of this book.

To be successful in this unit you have to understand:
- the key ideas of the content
- the nature of the assessment material — by reviewing and practising sample structured questions
- how to achieve a high level of performance within them

This guide has two sections:

Content Guidance — this summarises some of the key information that you need to know to be able to answer the examination questions with a high degree of accuracy and depth. In particular, the meaning of key terms is made clear and some attention is paid to providing details of case study material to help meet the spatial context requirement within the specification.

Questions & Answers — this includes some sample questions similar in style to those you might expect in the exam. There are some sample student responses to these questions as well as detailed analysis, which will give further guidance on what exam markers are looking for to award top marks.

The best way to use this book is to read through the relevant topic area first, before practising the questions. Only refer to the answers and examiner comments after you have attempted the questions.

Content Guidance

■ Health, human rights and intervention

What is human development and why do levels vary from place to place?

- Human development can be measured in a number of ways, including economic, environmental, health and human rights measures.
- Health varies considerably both within and between countries, and there are complex explanations for this.
- Health and development can be improved in different ways, involving different national and global organisations that have contrasting solutions.

Measuring development

The word 'development' is used to suggest that people are making progress. Traditionally this development progress has been measured using economic data, particularly:

- growth in the total GDP (Gross Domestic Product) of a country
- growth in **GDP per capita**
- a shift from traditional industries such as farming, towards manufacturing and the service sector

> **Exam tip**
>
> Recognise that the word 'development' has a complex meaning, including a narrowly economic one as well as much broader meanings linked to social progress.

These data measure economic development. **Human development** is a much broader concept. It can be measured using indices such as the Human Development Index (HDI). This combines data on income per person, life expectancy and education and so includes social aspects of progress as well as economic ones.

There are good reasons why focusing only on wealth in the context of development is a bad idea. Figure 1 shows the complex relationship between income and **life satisfaction**:

- life satisfaction increases rapidly with wealth when incomes are low to begin with
- when a medium level of income is reached, satisfaction increases only very slowly with additional income
- some people are much more satisfied than their income would suggest (Mexicans, Brazilians, Vietnamese) whereas others are much less satisfied (Japanese, Greeks, Turks)
- Nigerians, Russians and Japanese have similar levels of life satisfaction despite vastly different income levels

GDP per capita means average income per person: the value of all a country's goods and services produced in a year, divided by its population.

Human development is focused on progress in terms of people's quality of life, not just their wealth. It includes progress in freedom, equality and how content people are with their lives.

Life satisfaction, or human contentment, is how happy or satisfied people are with their lives. It is a measure of human wellbeing.

Knowledge check 1

On Figure 1, which countries have the highest and lowest life satisfaction?

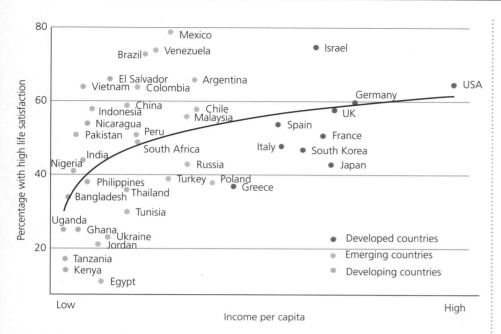

Adapted from Pew Global Research data

Figure 1 The relationship between income and life satisfaction

A relatively new measure of human development is the Happy Planet Index (HPI), introduced by the New Economics Foundation in 2006. It doesn't measure human 'happiness', but rather combines:

- **life expectancy**: a measure of human health
- **life satisfaction**: a measure of human contentment
- **ecological footprint**: a measure of the resources (energy, water, food) humans use

HPI is unusual in combining environmental data (ecological footprint) with social data on satisfaction and health — and *not* including data on income. Table 1 shows some results from the 2016 HPI. Countries that come out best using the HPI are neither developed nor developing — they are somewhere in the middle. It could be argued they balance human development with environmental management.

Table 1 Selected countries from the 2016 HPI

☹ Low HPI	☺ Medium HPI	☺ High HPI
USA, Russia, Ivory Coast, Chad, South Africa	Spain, India, UK, Indonesia, Brazil	Vietnam, Costa Rica, Mexico, Colombia, Thailand
Very wealthy but wasteful societies, or very poor developing countries — both very unequal	Very mixed group, but most lack extensive poverty and have good social conditions	Middle-income, emerging countries which balance quality of life and environment

Human development

There is no universal model for how a society should be run in order to maximise human contentment and levels of wealth. In most developed countries governments use taxes to fund a **welfare state** system that provides:

- free education, usually from age 4 or 5 to 16 or 18
- health services, which are free in some cases
- benefits such as a basic income, housing and social services to those in need

However, in developed countries there is large variation in terms of which benefits are provided, and how free and generous welfare state systems are. There are other models:

- In India, national and regional governments subsidise the costs of housing, food, fuel, fertilisers and water to make them effectively cheaper and affordable for low income people — at a cost of around US$60 billion per year.
- In Bolivia, since the election of President Evo Morales in 2006, taxes have been raised on the profits of oil **TNCs** to over 80% and the extra government income used to reduce poverty through health, education and other programmes including increasing the minimum wage by 50%.
- In Muslim countries, society is governed by **sharia law**. This includes the concept of *zakat*, which means the payment of taxes to help less fortunate people. Critics of Sharia argue it perpetuates gender inequality, by denying fundamental human rights to women.
- Professor Hans Rosling (1948–2017) stressed the crucial role health plays in human development, arguing that improving health, life expectancy and environmental quality often unlocks people's economic potential.

Both the Indian subsidy system and the radical tax redistribution of Evo Morales are seen by some as discouraging economic growth. This is because subsidies undercut some prices, and very high taxes discourage investment by TNCs. There is a general consensus that economic growth is important if human development is to increase long term.

Education and development

Education is very important to human development in a number of ways. Education increases the value of **human capital**. Most education comes from schooling (primary, secondary, university) but continues during employment (training). Table 2 shows the relationship between years in education and income for selected countries. The relationship works two ways.

- A low number of years in education means a poorly educated, unskilled workforce with low earning capacity, so incomes remain low.
- High incomes mean governments have the taxes to invest in education (investing in future human capital), which in turn drives up future income.

Table 2 Education and income data for selected countries (UN data)

	Expected years in education (2013)	Income per person (US$, 2016)
Norway	17.6	70,600
UK	16.2	40,250
Malaysia	12.7	9,500
India	11.7	1,700
Haiti	7.6	700
Niger	5.4	360

A **welfare state** promotes human wellbeing by redistributing resources to people in need such as children, the elderly, disabled, ill or unemployed.

TNCs are Transnational Corporations.

Sharia law is the legal system in most Muslim countries which dictates many aspects of life. It is applied differently across the Muslim world: strictly in some countries and more flexibly in others.

Exam tip

Make sure you learn examples of countries and people that have different interpretations of 'development' with different emphases.

Human capital is the value of knowledge, skills, judgement, creativity, training and experience within a society.

Knowledge check 2

In Table 2, what is the difference between the highest and lowest expected years of education?

While education is important to economic growth, it is also important in other ways. Higher levels of education contribute to a better understanding of **human rights**, and make it more likely people will assert their human rights if they are abused or undermined.

Education is not universal. It varies because of poverty (Table 2) but also in other ways. Most significantly, there are major gender inequalities in terms of access to education, as shown in Table 3.

■ In low-income sub-Saharan Africa, fewer girls than boys finish both primary and secondary school because education often costs money and boys are prioritised over girls.

■ Inequality is also clear in the Middle East and North Africa, especially in primary school: poverty plays a role but boys tend to be valued more than girls for religious and cultural reasons, so more boys finish school.

■ South Asia is a poor region, but education is valued highly and here girls get more schooling than boys.

Table 3 Gender inequalities in education

Global region	Primary school completion rate (%)		Secondary school completion rate (%)	
	Boys	Girls	Boys	Girls
Sub-Saharan Africa	72	66 (−6)	46	40 (−6)
Middle East and North Africa	93	87 (−6)	71	72 (+1)
EU	97	98 (+1)	89	86 (−3)
South Asia	92	94 (+2)	78	82 (+4)
Latin America	99	99 (0)	76	81 (+5)

Table 4 shows how, since 1970, the highest level of education achievement has improved dramatically in Africa but, even in 2020, 50% of 20–24 year olds are expected to leave education at the end of primary school and fewer than 10% will have had any post-secondary education.

Table 4 Trends in education achievement 1970–2020 (%)

Highest level of education achieved	Africa		North America	
	1970	2020	1970	2020
No education	59	22	2	0
Some primary	11	13	1	0
Completed primary	11	15	3	2
Some secondary	7	18	8	7
Completed secondary	8	23	65	67
Post-secondary	4	9	21	24

Human rights are the rights people are entitled to simply because they are human: they often include freedom, equality, the right to a fair trial, the right to education and a certain standard of living.

Exam tip

Modern discussions of development and social progress always consider gender issues and gender inequality, so having some data that relate to this is important.

Knowledge check 3

Which global region has the largest difference in primary and secondary school completion between boys and girls?

Developing world health and life expectancy

Health is important in terms of human development. Poor health can have a number of negative impacts that hinder development progress:

- childhood diseases can lead to stunting and poor cognitive development, affecting education later in life
- diseases such as malaria and HIV/Aids reduce capacity to work, and therefore earning capacity
- family members may have to spend long periods looking after ill relatives (rather than working), because health services are poor
- medical costs use up income that could be spent on food, education and housing

Table 5 shows how life expectancy varies in developing countries, from 52 years in Nigeria to 79 in Cuba — a huge difference. This is only partly explained by wealth differences:

- Cuba's life expectancy is the same as the USA's because Cuba has invested heavily in healthcare, water supply and **sanitation**, reducing disease — despite its relative poverty
- Ethiopia has high levels of **undernourishment**, which increases the risk of nutrition-related diseases such as scurvy and rickets, and increases susceptibility to infectious diseases
- low access to a safe water supply and poor sanitation spread water borne diseases such as cholera and dysentery

Nigeria's life expectancy is noticeably worse than Ethiopia's despite Nigeria being wealthier and having less undernourishment and better water supply and sanitation. Other factors, such as the high prevalence of malaria (11% of the population has been infected), poor access to doctors and the high risk of infectious diseases in densely packed slums in megacities such as Lagos, are important.

Table 5 Developing — and emerging — world health data

Country	Life expectancy	Income per capita (US$)	% population undernourished	% access to safe water supply	% access to sanitation
Cuba	79	7,800	2	95	91
India	67	1,700	15	88	44
Ethiopia	63	700	29	39	7
Nigeria	52	2,200	8	67	33

Comparing Table 5 with Table 6 shows how poor access to healthcare, combined with poor access to sanitation, water supply and food, impact on infant and **maternal mortality**. Poor access to healthcare is also a key issue.

Table 6 Infant and maternal mortality

Country	Infant mortality (per 1,000 live births)	Maternal mortality (per 100,000 live births)
Cuba	5	39
India	25	174
Ethiopia	51	353
Nigeria	71	814

Sanitation refers to systems for safely disposing of human waste, i.e. toilets, sewers and hand-washing facilities, all of which reduce infectious disease risk.

Undernourishment exists when food supply and calorie intake are inadequate, leading to health problems such as stunting in children; it is a type of malnutrition.

Maternal mortality is the number of women who die during, or shortly after, giving birth. It is measured as deaths per 100,000 live births.

Developed-world health and life expectancy

Life expectancy also varies within developed countries (Figure 2). The differences are not so large as in the developing world but they are significant: the average Japanese person can expect 13 more years than the average Russian. The variations are explained by a number of factors.

- **Lifestyle**: inactive lifestyles, combined with high fat/sugar diets, have contributed to 31% of adults in the UAE and 36% in the USA being obese, with high levels of diabetes and heart disease, which lowers life expectancy. Alcoholism is a serious problem in Russia, especially among men.

- **Diet**: the Japanese and South Korean diets contain more fish, vegetables and rice than Western diets, which are high in meat protein, fat and sugar. Better diet may lead to lower levels of cancer, heart disease and skeletal/joint illnesses such as osteoporosis and arthritis.

- **Deprivation**: about 40% of people in Bulgaria are at risk from poverty, despite its EU membership.

- **Medical care**: some countries, such as the UK, provide free healthcare for all (the NHS), which increases life expectancy. In the USA most people need expensive insurance policies to cover health costs, which many cannot afford. In Russia and Bulgaria, medical care is much less modern than in other developed countries and therefore less effective.

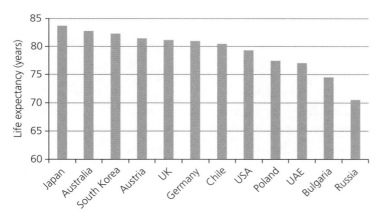

Source: UN WHO data

Figure 2 Life expectancy in developed countries, 2015

Exam tip

The specification has a significant focus on life expectancy and good answers will include specific life expectancy data on this topic.

Health within countries

Perhaps surprisingly, there are large variations in health and life expectancy *within* countries, even ones with universal, free healthcare systems such as the UK. In the UK, male life expectancy at birth is around 73 years in Glasgow, but 83 in the Isle of Purbeck in Dorset. This is similar in scale to the difference between being born in Bangladesh and Japan. In some small areas of Glasgow, male life expectancy is around 65. Blackpool (75), Middlesbrough (76) and Liverpool (76) also have male life expectancy rates lower than the national average of 79.5 years for men. There are many reasons for this:

- in deprived, **post-industrial** cities male unemployment is high, incomes low and levels of smoking and alcohol consumption are higher than the national average

Post-industrial cities are ones, such as Liverpool and Glasgow, in which traditional manufacturing industry has closed, leading to high unemployment, especially among males.

- diet among low-income groups is often poor, with cheap, high-fat fast-food consumed rather than fresh fruit and vegetables
- the combination of low income and poor lifestyle leads to high levels of heart disease, diabetes, some cancers, liver and kidney failure — and hence lower life expectancy

Inequality in health and life expectancy can also result from ethnic differences:

- Australians with European ancestry live nearly 20 years longer than **Aboriginal people**
- in New Zealand, the white European population live 11 years longer than indigenous Maoris

The root cause of these differences is poverty. Many Australian Aborigines and Maori live in isolated rural communities and have low-paid jobs. Levels of alcohol consumption, smoking and drug abuse are high. Food can be expensive in isolated communities, and access to healthcare is basic.

Aboriginal people are in the original inhabitants of Australia. They are called Maori in New Zealand.

> ### Knowledge check 4
> Which area of the UK has the lowest life expectancy?

Exam tip

Make sure you are clear about differences in life expectancy between developing and developed countries, as well as within countries.

Governments and social progress

Social progress is the idea that societies can improve over time in economic, human and environmental terms, and that governments play a key role in this. Government decisions can prioritise:

- economic development, through infrastructure spending, e.g. roads, railways, power grids and tax breaks to attract foreign investment
- human development through spending on education, healthcare and benefits for disadvantaged groups, and promoting freedom and equality
- environmental wellbeing, by reducing pollution (and its negative health effects), ensuring clean water and sanitation, and protecting ecosystems and species

Most governments do all of these things, but not equally. The Social Progress Index (SPI) attempts to quantify how well governments provide for their people. It is based on three factors:

1 **basic human needs**: nutrition, medical care, shelter, water, sanitation and safety
2 **foundations of wellbeing**: education, access to internet and mobile phones, life expectancy, pollution levels
3 **opportunity**: personal rights, political freedom, gender equality, tolerance of immigrants and access to advanced education

Table 7 explores the SPI for four countries. It is noticeable that:

- the democratic countries of Sweden and Costa Rica spend large sums, in relation to income per capita, on health and education, and this leads to high SPI scores because of the impact of a welfare state
- **authoritarian** Russia and Ethiopia are run by elites, who provide far less to their people and hence SPI scores are low

Authoritarian (or totalitarian) regimes are undemocratic governments and people cannot freely choose their leaders, and so cannot influence policy or freely criticise policies.

Table 7 SPI scores and government social spending data for four countries (2017 data)

Russia			Costa Rica		
79	72	50	88	85	71
Income per person: $10,600 Health spending: $524 per person/year Education spending: 4.1%			Income per person: $11,700 Health spending: $929 per person/year Education spending: 6.3%		
Moderate to low SPI scores. Health spending around half of Costa Rica's and education less than 2% of GDP. An authoritarian regime			Country with no armed forces. Government spends large sums on both health and education. SPI scores much higher than Russia, despite similar incomes. A functioning democracy		
Sweden			**Ethiopia**		
95	90	83	52	54	29
Income per person: $53,200 Health spending: $5,600 per person/year Education spending: 7%			Income per person: $870 Health spending: $24 per person/year Education spending: 4.5%		
Government with a strong commitment to welfare state spending, with high levels of both health and education provision provided by the government. An advanced democracy			Very low-income country, with low levels of spending on education and health. Very low SPI opportunity score. An authoritarian regime		

SPI scores (all out of 100) ▨ Basic needs ▨ Foundations of wellbeing ▨ Opportunity

Knowledge check 5

Which countries in Table 7 are democracies?

Neo-liberal views are those in favour of free-market capitalism and freedom for private businesses to trade and earn profits; neo-liberals are in favour of a reduced role for government in a country's economy.

IGOs (inter-governmental organisations) are regional or global organisations of which countries are members; they manage aspects of the economy, global development and specific issues such as health or environmental issues.

The role of IGOs

Many countries operate within what might be called a **neo-liberal** economic consensus. This means that economic development is focused on:

- free-trade between countries, with no or only very small barriers to free-trade such as import and export taxes, or quotas on the volume of imports
- the privatisation of government-owned industries, so that they are sold to private companies and run to maximise profit
- deregulation of capital markets, meaning money can flow easily and quickly between banks, businesses and countries

This consensus is supported by the work of **IGOs**, such as those shown in Table 8.

Table 8 IGOs and economic development

World Bank (WB)	World Trade Organization (WTO)	International Monetary Fund (IMF)
Part of the United Nations, the WB lends money to emerging and developing countries to promote development. It funds projects such as roads, hydro-electric power, telecoms and water supply schemes	The WTO promotes free trade through negotiations between countries. Since the 1950s a series of negotiating rounds have removed barriers to trade, although further progress has been limited since the 1990s	The IMF promotes global economic stability, by intervening in countries that experience economic difficulties. Its aim is to reduce the risk of market crashes and recessions

While the neo-liberal consensus is strong, there are concerns that it:

- benefits businesses and TNCs far more than ordinary people, and so creates inequality, i.e. a growing gap between rich and poor
- focuses on industrialisation, trade and jobs that tend to concentrate in cities, so rural areas miss out on economic growth and development

- focuses on profit and economic growth at the expense of the environment

Because of these concerns IGOs and **BINGOs** have also put in place programmes that have a greater social and environmental focus (Table 9).

Table 9 Global IGO and BINGO programmes

Environmental quality		Health	
Global Environment Facility (GEF) is a funding mechanism for environmental projects, that has raised US$17 billion since 1992 and attracted over US$80 billion more from private individuals and businesses		The Global Fund to Fight AIDS, Tuberculosis and Malaria was set up in Geneva in 2002. By 2016 it had raised and spent US$30 billion fighting disease in developing countries	
Education		Human rights	
In 2016 UNICEF's education programme reached 15.7 million children in over 330,000 classrooms, provided training in 39,000 schools and supported 11.7 million children in crisis situations, such as refugees		The Global Fund for Human Rights is an NGO focused on human rights since 2003, and has provided US$85 million in grants to over 600 human rights groups worldwide	

BINGO is an acronym for big, international non-governmental organisation. These are large global NGOs that raise funds worldwide and assist people in many countries at the same time.

UN MDGs and SDGs

A global response to lack of development progress in South Asia and Africa in particular was the adoption of the United Nations Millennium Development Goals (**MDGs**) that ran from 2000 to 2015. The MDGs consisted of eight global goals and subsidiary targets (Table 10).

The **MDGs** (Millennium Development Goals) were goals and targets set by the United Nations to improve the lives of people living in developing countries.

Table 10 Selected MDG goals

Halve the proportion of people living on less than US$1.25 a day	Halve the proportion of people who suffer from hunger	By 2015, all children can complete a full course of primary schooling, girls and boys
Eliminate gender disparity in primary and secondary education, preferably by 2005 and at all levels by 2015	Reduce by two-thirds the under-five mortality rate	Reduce by three-quarters the maternal mortality ratio

Exam tip

Exam questions focusing on the MDGs will look back at development progress already made, whereas ones on the SDGs topic are likely to look forward.

The MDGs were ambitious goals and targets, focused on meeting basic needs in terms of health, income, food supply, water and sanitation. How successful were they? Estimates suggest:

- the health targets prevented 20 million deaths between 2000 and 2015
- infant mortality in sub-Saharan Africa fell by 53%
- numbers living in extreme poverty fell from 1.7 billion in 2000 to 0.8 billion in 2015
- undernourishment fell from 20% to 13% between 2000 and 2015
- primary school enrolment increased from 83% to 91%
- maternal mortality fell from 330 to 210 deaths per 100,000 live births

Although these data suggest success, there are problems. Some countries, especially China, account for a huge slice of this 'success' and this risks masking more limited progress in some parts of South Asia and Africa. East Asia and Latin America have made better progress than other developing regions. Gender inequality has not improved as much as hoped, and conflict in many countries (Somalia, Yemen, DRC) has set progress back. By 2015, 800 million people still lived in extreme poverty and hunger, and 800 million lived in slum housing in cities.

The **SDGs** replaced the MDGs for the period 2015–30. They too set targets for basic needs, but in addition they have a focus on **sustainable development**, including:

- clean energy, i.e. renewable/low-carbon energy
- decent work, i.e. for a decent wage and avoiding exploitation
- sustainable cities, for the more than 50% of the world's population living in urban areas
- protecting oceans and ecosystems

Why do human rights vary from place to place?

- Human rights are an important concept in international law, and are recognised as an international norm protected by international agreements and treaties.
- Human rights are a contested concept, and they are not universally protected in all nation states.
- Within countries human rights are not universal — they can vary because of gender and ethnicity, with serious consequences for some groups.

Universal Declaration of Human Rights

The term 'human rights' dates to the eighteenth century, although the concept of certain rights — such as the right to life and freedom — is a much older one. Precursors to the modern concept of human rights can be found in:

- the English Bill of Rights, 1689
- the United States Declaration of Independence, 1777
- the French Declaration of the Rights of the Man and of the Citizen, 1789

These documents asserted the idea that people are born free, and that governments should be elected freely and that property cannot be confiscated from people by those in power. The idea of a free and fair trial was also important. These historical documents often focused on the rights of property-owning men, and had much less to say about the rights of women, slaves and peasants.

> **Exam tip**
>
> There is no need to learn the UDHR or ECHR off by heart, but you do need to know the key human rights principles each contains.

In 1948 the United Nations adopted the Universal Declaration of Human Rights (UDHR) in order to make the human rights specified in the 1945 United Nations Charter more clearly defined (Table 11). The UDHR was largely a response to the **Holocaust** inflicted by the Nazis during the Second World War, to ensure such actions were never repeated. Since its adoption, the UDHR has been used:

The **SDGs** are the Sustainable Development Goals: 17 global goals that apply to all countries, not just developing countries as with the MDGs.

Sustainable development is 'development that meets the needs of the present without compromising the ability of future generations to meet their own needs' as defined by Gro Harlem Brundtland in 1987.

Knowledge check 6

Which type of countries did the MDGs apply to, and which do the SDGs apply to?

Human rights are shared principles or values, which some argue are universal, giving humans certain rights that should never be denied. They set standards of human behaviour by being made into laws — either at a national or international level.

The **Holocaust** refers to the persecution and killing of Jews (and Roma people, the disabled, gay men, Slavs and others) under the Nazi Germany regime, which led to the deaths of up to 17 million people.

- to place political pressure on countries seen to be denying people basic human rights, and press for change
- as a justification for economic sanctions against countries
- as a justification for military intervention in foreign countries seen to be committing genocide or widespread human rights abuses

The UDHR is an important document in foreign policy because it informs the actions of countries towards other sovereign states.

Table 11 The Universal Declaration of Human Rights

Articles 1–2	Articles 3–11	Articles 12–17
Fundamental rights of dignity, liberty and equality	The right to life, and the banning of slavery. Prohibition of torture. The right to a free and fair trial	The right to freedom of movement. The right to asylum. The right to own property
Articles 18–21	**Articles 22–27**	**Articles 28–30**
Freedom of thought, political opinion and religion	The right to health and a decent standard of living. The right to education	These deal with the application of human rights

Only the 58 countries that were members of the UN in 1948 voted on the UDHR (48 in favour, 8 abstentions and 2 non-votes). Countries that have joined the UN since 1948 have agreed to it as they joined. However, some subsequent human rights agreements have not been adopted by all UN member states:

- the USA has not **ratified** the 1990 UN Convention on the Rights of the Child
- China and Cuba have not ratified the 1976 UN International Covenant on Civil and Political Rights
- over 50 countries have not signed, or have only partly adopted the 1981 Convention on the Elimination of all Forms of Discrimination Against Women

European Convention on Human Rights

In Europe there is a further human rights treaty called the European Convention on Human Rights (ECHR). This:

- was written by the **Council of Europe** and adopted by its 47 member states
- pre-dates the founding of the EU in 1957, and was signed in 1950 coming into force in 1953
- established the European Court of Human Rights to uphold the ECHR and bring people or organisations abusing human rights to trial and justice

The ECHR was specifically set up to prevent conflict in Europe and prevent the sort of atrocities committed against people during the two World Wars. The text of the ECHR is different to that of the United Nations UDHR but the two documents have very similar aims and the rights they refer to are very similar.

In the UK, the Human Rights Act 1998 took the rights enshrined in the ECHR and made them part of UK law. This makes it easier for citizens to have their human rights upheld in the UK, rather than having to take the UK government to court at the European Court of Human Rights in Strasbourg.

A treaty or agreement signed at the UN only becomes legally binding when it is **ratified** by a member state. Ratification usually involves a vote in the parliament or legislature of that nation state.

The **Council of Europe** is an international organisation set up in 1949 with the specific aims of upholding human rights, democracy and the rule of law in Europe. It is not the same as the European Union, but has a close relationship with it.

The UDHR and ECHR are controversial to some people because of their impact on **sovereignty**.

- By signing international human rights treaties, sovereign states could be seen to be handing authority on human rights issues to a higher legal body, e.g. the UN or Council of Europe.
- In the case of the ECHR, the European Court of Human Rights in Strasbourg has a higher legal power to make judgements than national courts.

A wider, but related, issue is that some have criticised the concept of 'human rights' as being a Western one, i.e. put in place after the Second World War by European and North American politicians and thinkers. They argue that this Western concept of human rights does not apply easily to Islamic or Asian cultures which have different histories and traditions. The question of whether there are certain human rights that are **universal** is an interesting one. Different cultures may take a different view of gender equality, or treat some crimes less/more seriously than other cultures.

The Geneva Conventions

International law also governs actions during wartime. The Geneva Conventions have a history dating back to the 1860s. The current version is the Fourth Geneva Convention, signed by 196 countries in 1949. It has been updated since with various amendments called protocols. The Geneva Conventions cover the '**rules of war**' in the following ways:

- wounded and sick soldiers should be evacuated from the field of battle and given medical treatment, even by the enemy side
- prisoners should be well treated, not used for forced labour and hostages should not be taken
- civilians should be protected in areas that have been conquered

The Geneva Conventions helped define **war crimes**. Those accused of war crimes can be tried at the International Criminal Court (ICC) in The Hague, Netherlands set up in 2002. Recognition of the ICC by sovereign states is widespread (there are 123 signatories) but not universal (the USA, China, Russia and India do not recognise the ICCs status). There are difficulties with the ICC:

- international cooperation to bring war criminals to trial can be hard to achieve as not all states agree with it
- war criminals have to be captured and then brought to The Hague: those accused attempt to avoid this at all costs
- gathering evidence of war crimes during a war is very difficult

Since 2002 the ICC has investigated war crimes linked to 11 wars, and accused 42 individuals, of which 34 have had arrest warrants issued against them. As of 2018, only five war criminals have been convicted at the ICC.

Exam tip

Make sure you understand that the Geneva Conventions are much narrower in scope than the UDHR, as they only apply to conflict situations.

Sovereignty is the concept that a country's government determines the laws and policies in that country, and no higher authority has supreme power.

Knowledge check 8

Which court is responsible for passing judgements on the European Convention of Human Rights?

Universalism is a view that certain moral principles apply to all peoples, everywhere. The UDHR effectively takes this view, but this is disputed by some.

The **rules of war** govern acceptable conduct during a war, and recognise that in some cases war can be legally justified. However, it is widely accepted that there are limits to actions that can be taken during a war, such as widespread killing of civilians, use of chemical weapons or attempts at total destruction of people and property.

War crimes include intentional killing of prisoners, taking hostages, torture, rape, genocide, use of child soldiers, bombing civilians and use of chemical weapons during a conflict.

Content Guidance

A key issue with the Geneva Conventions, human rights law and the ICC is that many sovereign states still engage in actions that are banned by treaties and agreements that they have signed up to:

- Amnesty International, a human rights charity, estimates that 140 sovereign states use torture, for instance
- around 25 countries still possess chemical weapons
- by some definitions the USA has attempted regime change in over 30 countries since 1945, and many of these can be questioned under international law
- most sovereign states consider Russia's invasion and annexation of parts of Georgia (2008) and Ukraine (2014) illegal under international law

Protecting human rights

A number of countries are seen as being at the forefront of human rights, including all the Scandinavian countries, the Netherlands, France, Germany, the UK and Canada. These countries have signed up to all aspects of UN human rights agreements, and enshrined protection and equality relating to ethnicity, gender, sexuality, disability and children, and issues such as modern slavery and people trafficking into their own laws.

- These countries are considered 'free' using the Freedom House 'Freedom in the World Index' shown in Figure 3.
- They are usually the first countries to 'call out' human rights abuses.

Sweden, Finland, Norway, Austria, Ireland and Switzerland are historically neutral countries. This has meant that they are often the locations chosen for making international agreements on human rights, and their diplomats are often involved in negotiating agreements and settling disputes.

The 'unfree' and 'partly free' countries shown on Figure 3, in some cases, prioritise economic growth over human rights. This includes China, Malaysia, Mexico, much of the Middle East and large parts of Africa. It could be argued that:

- human rights bring financial costs, such as providing education and healthcare, and this money can be better spent on economic infrastructure
- workers rights get in the way of profits, because they add costs to businesses
- rights such as freedom of the press bring no economic benefits

On the other hand, people may be much more productive and innovative when they have the protected freedoms that human rights bring. It is of course noticeable that many of the world's wealthiest countries are also the ones with the best human rights records.

Countries such as China defend their position by arguing that once economic development is achieved, human rights may well follow. They would argue that in the UK gender equality, the universal right to vote, universal healthcare and education all emerged *after* our industrial revolution not before or during it.

Knowledge check 9

What does the International Criminal Court in The Hague investigate?

Regime change refers to a situation when one or more countries attempt to change the government/leadership of another sovereign state using military intervention and/or political and economic pressure.

Neutral countries do not take sides in conflicts, and intend to be neutral in future conflicts. In many cases, neutral countries do not join military alliances (but they usually do have their own armed forces).

3

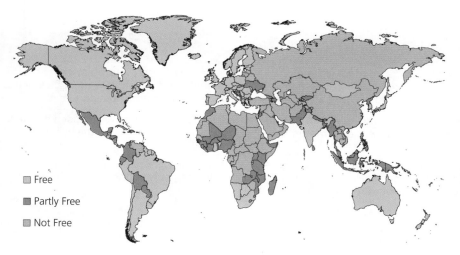

■ Free

■ Partly Free

■ Not Free

Figure 3 The Freedom in the World Index, 2018

Democratic freedom

A key aspect of human rights is that of democracy. A democratic political system allows the people to vote out of office a government that is doing a bad job. Democracy is surprisingly rare (Figure 4) according to the Economist Intelligence Unit (EIU). It groups 163 countries into four categories:

- **full democracy**: civil liberties and political freedoms fully respected and protected (Norway, UK, Canada)
- **flawed democracy**: elections are fair and civil liberties are protected but there are problems, e.g. the media may not be free (South Korea, South Africa, USA, India)
- **hybrid regimes**: elections are not free and fair, the legal system is not independent of government and corruption is widespread (Turkey, Bangladesh)
- **authoritarian regimes**: dictatorship, or systems where elections are meaningless; civil liberties abuses are common and the legal system is not independent. Media censored (Russia, China, Saudi Arabia)

In hybrid and authoritarian countries **freedom of speech** is usually not respected at all. Table 12 compares human rights in China — an authoritarian regime — with those in India, which is considered a flawed democracy. Despite India's apparent positive record shown in Table 12, there are human rights problems in India related to the **caste system**, lack of rights among Muslim women and lack of LGBT rights.

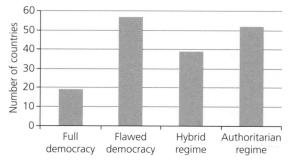

Figure 4 The 2017 EIU Democracy Index

Exam tip

Learn some examples of countries with different degrees of democractic freedom.

Freedom of speech is the right to express opinions without fear of persecution, censorship or retaliation: in democracies it is fiercely protected, but there are often some restrictions to prevent incitement of violence or hate speech.

The Indian **caste system** is a hereditary form of social hierarchy, which limits lower caste groups in terms of types of jobs they can have and therefore their income. It is a form of discrimination. Although the system has weakened, lower caste groups are still subject to abuse.

Knowledge check 10

According to Figure 4, which type of political system is the least common in the world?

Table 12 Human rights in India and China

	India (Flawed democracy)	China (Authoritarian)
Religious freedom	Despite religious freedom, religious violence and intolerance is common between Hindu, Muslim and Sikh groups	Christianity is barely tolerated, and Communist Party members must be atheists. Buddhism and Islam are suppressed
Freedom of speech	Generally upheld: anti-government and single-issue protests are common, but police violence is also common	'Subversion of state power' is used to crack down on dissenting voices; the internet is censored
Political freedom	There are around 2,000 political parties in India, and its hotly contested elections are the largest democratic ones in the world	The Chinese Communist Party is, in practice, the only political party that exists
Freedom of the press	There are numerous, privately owned media organisations that have reduced the influence of government	Not free. Media are monitored by the Communist Party and subject to government direction

There has been some movement by emerging countries towards democracy, for instance South Korea transitioned to democracy in 1987, Chile in 1989 and Brazil in 1985. Other emerging countries — such as China and Turkey — have not moved in this way.

Political corruption

Human rights depend on having people in power who are prepared to protect those rights. Perhaps the most important aspect of this is having an independent **judiciary** that is not interfered with by politicians and cannot be 'bought' by people with power and money. An independent judiciary is a key principle of democratic government, referred to as separation of powers between those who make laws (government) and those that apply them (judiciary).

The judiciary is undermined by **corruption** because the rule of law can be subverted by corruption:

- judges can be bribed to dismiss legitimate human rights abuse cases, perhaps by wealthy business owners or TNCs
- the appointment of judges can be influenced by politicians, rather than them being appointed independently
- corrupt politicians can steal government money, or foreign aid, so it cannot be used as intended to improve human rights.

The overall impact of corruption is usually to create an untouchable group of powerful, wealthy people supported by a corrupt judicial system. Ordinary people are then left with no means of having their human rights upheld, so human rights abuses are widespread. Inevitably, countries with high levels of corruption (as measured by indices such as Transparency International's Corruption Perceptions Index (CPI)), are those with the worst track records on human rights.

Gender and ethnic differences

Human rights vary widely between sovereign states, but also within them. This is particularly the case in post-colonial states that gained their independence from European colonial powers in the period 1945–80.

The **judiciary** in a sovereign state is the court system or judicial system that applies laws passed by the government and in some cases may judge that laws passed by government are illegal.

Corruption is the misuse of public power for private benefit.

Exam tip

The role of the judiciary is especially important in human rights, as it is usually courts and judges that uphold human rights. Make sure you understand this role.

Human rights in these countries have proved problematic because:

- human rights had almost no role in colonial governance, so there was little history of respecting such rights
- post-colonial governments were often weak, and in many cases authoritarian
- post-colonial poverty led to a focus on economic growth, and basic needs, but not human rights
- post-colonial national borders rarely reflected the geography of nations of people, meaning many countries contained religious and/or ethnic minority groups that were ignored or even persecuted by the majority.

Table 13 summarises two situations where minority groups have been denied human rights.

Table 13 Ethnicity and gender human rights disparities

The Rohingya people in Myanmar	Women in Pakistan
Myanmar was the British colony of Burma until 1948	Pakistan was part of British India until Indian partition and independence in 1947
■ The Rohingya are a Muslim nation living in Rakhine State in northwest Myanmar — a majority Buddhist country ■ Under the 1982 Myanmar Nationality Law the Rohingya were denied nationality — meaning they had no rights and were effectively stateless ■ In 1978, 1991–92, 2012 and 2015–18 military crackdowns and persecution forced thousands of Rohingya to flee as refugees to nearby Bangladesh ■ The 2015–18 crisis has been called a genocide and crime against humanity	■ Despite the adoption of laws to protect women's rights in Pakistan, and some progress in improving women's lives, progress has been very slow ■ Despite being illegal, child marriage is still common ■ Forced marriage is widespread ■ Female literacy is around 45%, compared with 70% for men ■ Honour killings of women are still common in parts of Pakistan, and despite this being murder are often ignored or very lightly punished

Health and education

The lack of human rights among women and minority religious/ethnic groups has a direct influence on quality of life. Many countries have laws that in theory should protect such groups and prevent discrimination, but these are widely ignored. This combines with prejudice among the wider population to deny access to key services and opportunities (housing, employment, education, healthcare) to these groups. Table 14 shows differences between the **indigenous** population of the USA and the population as a whole. It is clear that American Indian and Alaskan Native peoples are poorer, less well educated and live shorter lives than the wider US population.

Table 14 Indigenous versus wider USA population (2015 data; source: US Census Bureau)

	American Indian & Alaskan Natives	USA population as a whole
Own home	53%	63%
High school diploma	83%	87%
Average income	$38,500	$55,750
Households in poverty	27%	15%
No health insurance	21%	9%
Life expectancy	73 years	79 years

Exam tip

Learn some examples of human rights abuses, as use of located examples is important in essay questions.

Honour killings occur when women are murdered by family members, because they are seen to have brought 'shame' on the family in some way (such as an extra-marital affair). The murder is seen as 'restoring the family honour'.

Knowledge check 11

What were the Rohingya people in Myanmar denied in 1982, making them effectively stateless people?

Indigenous people are the original population of an area, who were present in an area before the arrival of immigrants from elsewhere in the world — usually white European colonisers in the period 1500–1900.

In Latin America there are around 45 million indigenous people, around 8% of the total population of the region. Many live in rural areas of Latin America, and a small number still lead an isolated, tribal lifestyle in places such as the Amazon Basin. Indigenous groups frequently lack access to services and opportunities, and also suffer discrimination because of ethnicity. Table 15 compares the health and education of indigenous and non-indigenous groups: the latter are largely ethnically white, as they are descendants of European immigrants. In all cases in Table 15, the health and education provision is worse for indigenous groups.

Table 15 Indigenous and non-indigenous health and education data for Latin American countries (2011–12 data; source: UN and World Bank)

Brazil	Indigenous women with 13 years of education (%)	14
	Non-indigenous women with 13 years of education (%)	27
Bolivia	Contraceptive use among indigenous women (%)	56
	Contraceptive use among non-indigenous women (%)	69
Peru	Indigenous infant mortality (per 1,000 live births)	38
	Non-indigenous infant mortality (per 1,000 live births)	11
Mexico	Indigenous births attended by skilled medical staff (%)	81
	Non-indigenous births attended by skilled medical staff (%)	98

Exam tip

Try to use the term 'indigenous people' or refer to specific groups by name, and avoid terms such as 'native people'.

Demands for equality

Differences in human rights do lead to real differences in income, education, health and opportunity between different groups, even within the same country. This inequality is widely seen as unfair and unjustifiable. It has led to demands for equality especially from women and ethnic minority groups. However, progress towards equality has often been slow.

- **Australia**: Aboriginal and Torres Strait Islander Australians were only counted in the national census, and allowed to vote, in 1967. Starting in 1976, some land rights have been granted to indigenous people so they have title to some of their traditional lands. However, Aboriginal and Torres Strait Islander Australians still feel under-represented in politics and business, and feel their rights (especially rights to land) have not been met. Their life expectancy is nearly 10 years less than white Australians.

- **Bolivia**: the election of Evo Morales as Bolivian President in 2006 brought rapid changes for indigenous people in the country. Morales is indigenous himself, and his policies have been targeted at reducing discrimination against his people. Land reform, education reform to get indigenous youth into university, a literacy campaign, benefits for those in poverty and increased health spending have all improved wellbeing for indigenous groups — but some argue they have made the middle class worse off, as well as discouraging investment because taxes on businesses are very high.

- **Afghanistan**: women lack equality in most Islamic countries, but perhaps no more so than in Afghanistan. Progress in women's education and participation was made between 1973 and 1992, but was dramatically reversed when the **Taliban** took power in 1996: women could not go out alone, appear on TV, be visible in a house from the street, be employed or even get medical attention. Since 2001, limited progress has again been made with a more moderate government in charge, but the position of women is no better than it was in the 1970s.

Knowledge check 12

What is the difference in life expectancy between American Indian and Alaskan Natives and the wider US population?

The **Taliban** are a fundamentalist religious and political group, observing an extremely strict version of Sharia law which treats women with brutality. They were the effective government of Afghanistan, 1996–2001.

How are human rights used as arguments for political and military interventions?

- Human rights abuses can lead to interventions by Western governments, inter-governmental organisations and non-governmental organisations.
- Development aid and investment may improve human rights but their track record is mixed and in some cases human rights are ignored in favour of economic goals.
- Military interventions have complex justifications, including human rights issues, and do not always improve the human rights situation.

Geopolitical interventions

Interference by one sovereign state in the affairs of another is not new. In 1827 Great Britain, Russia and France intervened in Greece to force the Ottoman Empire (modern-day Turkey) to give Greece its independence. This intervention was justified on **humanitarian grounds** in order to end Ottoman brutality and free the Greeks from Ottoman rule.

Interventions take a variety of forms, some of which are high risk because they involve the use of force. Table 16 summarises the range of interventions used to promote development and address human rights issues.

Humanitarian grounds is a justification for an action based on ending violations of human rights.

Intervention means an action taken by one or more sovereign states, within the territory of another sovereign state, in order to change the political and social conditions in that place.

Table 16 Types of geopolitical interventions

Development aid	<ul><li>Money, technical help or physical supplies (equipment, food and medicine) provided from one country to another, often involving IGOs such as the UN and/or NGOs</li><li>Aid aims to improve quality of life by meeting basic needs (food, clean water, education and healthcare)</li></ul>
Trade embargoes	<ul><li>Otherwise known as economic sanctions, they prevent a country undertaking international trade in the normal way</li><li>By preventing exports, or banning imports, pressure is placed on the leaders of a sovereign state to change policy because their economy suffers</li></ul>
Military aid	<ul><li>Money provided from one sovereign state to another to buy military equipment</li></ul>
Indirect military action	<ul><li>Military equipment, or military advisers, are provided from one sovereign state to another (or another military group within it)</li><li>This is usually done in support of one side in a civil conflict</li></ul>
Direct military action	<ul><li>Armed forces from one sovereign state engaging in conflict in another sovereign state</li><li>This is often done as part of a coalition, i.e. several countries acting collectively</li></ul>

> **Exam tip**
>
> 'Intervention' is a broad term: make sure you specify the type of intervention you mean in your exam answers.

Governments, IGOs and NGOs

The legal case for intervention is complex:

- international law normally prohibits one sovereign state intervening in the internal affairs of another
- it can take place if the state being intervened in has committed an act of aggression on another sovereign state

■ however, the UN Charter and UDHR provide grounds for intervention without external aggression, if human rights abuses are widespread and there is a **humanitarian crisis**

■ the **UN Security Council** can authorise intervention if all five permanent members of the Security Council agree

The UN effectively has the *right* to intervene to protect people, although there is a view — called 'responsibility to protect' — that argues that organisations such as the UN have a *responsibility* to intervene. This view is more proactive, and would lead to more interventions than is currently the case.

In the twenty-first century human rights violations are front-page news. The internet, mobile phone cameras, social media and platforms such as YouTube mean human rights abuses can be documented and publicised like never before. There are several NGOs that campaign solely on human rights issues (Table 17).

Table 17 NGOs campaigning for human rights

Name	Founded	HQ	Organisation
Amnesty International	1961	London	A mass-membership organisation funded by members and supporters, that promotes direct action such as protests, letter writing and campaigning
Human Rights Watch	1978	New York	Largely funded by wealthy individuals, it puts pressure on governments to take action and intervene

There is often widespread agreement between governments, NGOs and IGOs, such as the UN, that human rights abuses have occurred, such as:

■ the 2015–18 Rohingya refugee crisis in Myanmar, involving the persecution of the Muslim Rohingya nation in Rakhine State by the Myanmar government military forces

■ the Bosnian genocide of Muslim men and boys that took place during the 1992–95 Bosnian War, and the genocide of the Tutsi in Rwanda by Hutu forces in 1994

■ the forced seclusion and ill-treatment of women during the Taliban regime in Afghanistan 1996–2001

However, there is often disagreement about the scale of the abuses and the extent to which they justify intervention. Even when the case for 'doing something' is very strong, intervention may not happen because no **consensus** can be found:

■ NGOs have little power to intervene, unless they are invited to do so by a sovereign state, or they are protected by the forces of another

■ the UN has no military forces of its own: it relies on member states providing and funding these

■ geography might make intervention technically very difficult: land-locked countries, dense jungle, lack of air-strips to land personnel and supplies

A **humanitarian crisis** is an event, or number of events, that threatens the health, safety and wellbeing of large numbers of people.

The **UN Security Council** is a 15-member UN body charged with maintaining international peace and security. Its five permanent members are the USA, Russia, China, the UK and France. There are also ten temporary members (member states take turns on a rotating basis).

Knowledge check 13

How many members of the UN Security Council are there?

Consensus means widespread agreement, i.e. that action should be taken. It may not be unanimous, but enough players agree to make it possible.

- geopolitical considerations may prevent intervention. These include the risks that intervention could lead to wider conflict, or different sides in a conflict being allied to opposing powerful countries, e.g. the USA and Russia

Intervention and national sovereignty

In most situations the intervention of one sovereign state in the affairs of another is considered illegal under international law. Intervention breaches the principle of sovereignty which is itself a crucial element of international law and the operation of the United Nations. The concept of sovereignty is important: it means the legal right to govern a physical territory. Sovereignty has four aspects:

1 a government, organised within a territory, has authority over that territory
2 the government controls movement of people and goods across the territory's borders
3 the government and territory is recognised by other governments
4 other organisations, outside the territory, do not have higher authority

Any intervention by other sovereign states breaches these aspects of sovereignty. In practice this usually means the 'bar' for intervention is high: there needs to be very strong moral and ethical grounds for direct military intervention, e.g. widespread and serious human rights violations.

Western governments do intervene, indirectly, in the affairs of other sovereign states by using economic levers to apply pressure. This is done in two main ways:

1 offering **aid** to help economic and social development, but attaching conditions (with 'strings attached') that seek to improve some aspect of human rights, such as the education of women and girls, or strengthening the rights of a minority group
2 negotiating trade agreements such as lower import tariffs or removing import quotas, but on the condition that human rights are improved

There are two ways of looking at this type of action:

1 it could be seen in a positive way as an 'ethical foreign policy', i.e. using the power of aid and trade to improve the lives of people in developing countries by strengthening their human rights
2 it could be seen as interference in the sovereign affairs on another country, by effectively forcing the country to change internal policies in order to gain a benefit from another country

The situation with aid is interesting. Figure 5 shows the top ten recipients of development aid from the UK and USA in 2017.

- There is considerable overlap in the lists: countries experiencing conflict or terrorism (Afghanistan, Syria, Pakistan), coping with refugee crises (Jordan — refugees from Syria) or poor, large, strategically important sub-Saharan African countries (Tanzania, Ethiopia, Nigeria) all get large sums in aid.
- None of the top ten recipients are democracies or flawed democracies based on the EIU Democracy Index.
- The sums of money involved are large: the USA gave a total of US$16 billion in development aid in 2017 (and a further, separate US$10 billion in military aid).

Knowledge check 14

Which countries are the Rohingya Muslims fleeing from, and fleeing to?

Exam tip

Make sure you revise a range of examples of interventions, which will be more useful than a small number of long case studies.

Aid is often used as short-hand for 'foreign aid', or technically Official Development Assistance (ODA) — meaning money (grants or loans) or technical help/equipment given from a donor country to a recipient to help economic and social development.

In sub-Saharan Africa, UK and USA aid is targeted at developing countries, and may improve human rights through meeting basic needs (education, health, food, water and shelter) but it is also about geopolitical influence by creating allies, fighting threats such as terrorism and countering influences from elsewhere — such as from Russia and China.

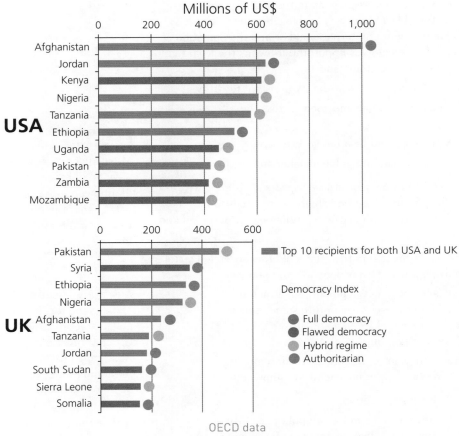

Figure 5 USA and UK development aid in 2017

Exam tip

Development aid is big business and the sums of money involved are huge, so learn some key data to quote as evidence in your answers.

Knowledge check 15

From which continent are six of the UK's top ten development aid recipients?

Development aid

Developed countries provide developing and emerging countries with about US$150 billion of aid each year. This money is targeted at improving human welfare and human rights. Aid takes many forms, as shown in Table 18.

Table 18 Types of aid

Bilateral aid	Multilateral aid	Aid from NGOs	Emergency aid
Given from one country to another, either as cash grants, loans, technical or military equipment	Given from an IGO, such as the World Bank. This often involves loans, which have to be repaid	Provided by charities such as Oxfam and Christian Aid, funded by donations from ordinary people	Short-term aid, to cope with a natural disaster such as an earthquake or epidemic. This is often from NGOs and governments

Aid donors — the countries and organisations that give development aid — may have complex motives for providing it, including:

- a genuine desire to improve human rights and human welfare
- political ties, such as providing aid to ex-colonies — which may involve an element of guilt or responsibility for past exploitation
- as a way to gain economic access for businesses and assist with trade deals (or prevent other countries from gaining influence)
- as a way to strengthen political alliances

It is tempting to see development aid, in some cases, as amounting to economic 'bribery' if the donor's motives appear to be largely political and economic. However, the counter-argument is that development aid can have more than one aim, e.g. improving human welfare while at the same time strengthening alliances between donor and recipient.

Does aid work?

The question of whether development aid improves human rights and human welfare is a very difficult one. A key problem is that of corruption. Some development aid money never reaches the people it is intended to help because:

- it is stolen by corrupt government officials
- bribery siphons off some of the money, which is wasted on corrupt contracts costing far more than the real cost of goods
- aid money often goes to companies owned and run by government officials and local elites, making it easier to steal

It is impossible to know how much development aid is lost to corruption. It may be a larger problem with large-scale, high-cost bilateral and multilateral projects. NGOs are probably more able to control corruption because their sums are small, and tend to be spent very locally.

There is an argument that development aid actually promotes corruption. Some people may view it as essentially 'free money' which increases the temptation to get some of it through corrupt means. Others argue development aid has wider negative impacts because:

- it reduces innovation, free enterprise and entrepreneurship because it provides a basic level of economic support
- it creates **dependency**, so countries begin to rely on aid 'handouts' rather than fostering economic development

Dependency means an unhealthy reliance on others, reducing the ability of the dependant to act on their own.

Figure 6 shows that many African countries do indeed depend heavily on aid, which makes up a significant share of their overall annual national income. The counter-argument is that without development aid, human welfare would be much worse.

There have been some major development aid success stories, which show it would be wrong to dismiss aid as pointless (Table 19).

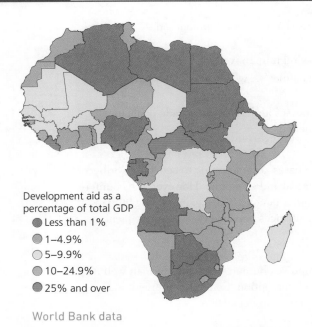

Development aid as a
percentage of total GDP

- Less than 1%
- 1–4.9%
- 5–9.9%
- 10–24.9%
- 25% and over

World Bank data

Figure 6 Development aid as a percentage of GDP in Africa, 2016

> **Exam tip**
>
> Many exam questions will require you to weigh-up the extent to which development aid, economic development or military intervention work: make sure you can provide arguments for and against.

Table 19 Development aid success stories

Global vaccination programmes	Tackling malaria	Women's education
■ Led by the UN World Health Organization since the 1960s, immunisation has dramatically reduced the disease burden in developing countries ■ Smallpox was eradicated in 1977, measles deaths fell by 85% in Africa from 2000 to 2014 and worldwide polio cases have fallen by 99% since 1988	■ The Bill and Melinda Gates Foundation, an NGO, has spent US$2 billion fighting malaria ■ Since 2005 new cases are down 25%, and deaths down 42% ■ Anti-mosquito bednets, better diagnosis and treatment, and improved insecticides have all contributed to controlling malaria and the mosquitoes that carry it	■ Under the umbrella of the Millennium Development Goals, progress has been made in gender equality ■ The global gap between male and female primary and secondary school enrolment was eliminated between 2000 and 2015 ■ Globally, more women are in work, and more involved in politics than in 2000

Economic development

Development aid can improve human rights and human welfare, but so can economic development. If businesses grow, they provide jobs and incomes and people's lives improve. The reduction in poverty in China from 88% of people in 1981 to 5% in 2018 was largely driven by job creation in cities, fuelled by foreign direct investment in Chinese industry.

However, in low-income, developing countries economic development is often focused on the **primary economic sector**. A number of players can undertake this, including:

- TNCs from developed countries, including oil and gas companies such as Shell and ExxonMobil
- government-owned companies (state-run enterprises) and agencies of developing countries
- **sovereign wealth funds** from developed and emerging countries

The **primary economic sector** includes farming, mining, forestry and fishing: it involves obtaining raw materials.

Sovereign wealth funds (SWFs) are government-owned investment funds. They invest national wealth in economic development projects, often overseas.

While activities such as drilling for oil, forestry and commercial farming can generate economic development they often involve:

- pollution, such as oil drilling spills and polluted waste water from mining
- deforestation from forestry and to make new farmland
- disregard for the land rights of local and indigenous people

This situation is made worse by the lack of environmental laws and monitoring, lack of clear **land title**, and corruption which allows illegal and damaging activities to continue unchecked in some developing countries. Table 20 summarises the impacts of two types of economic development in Africa.

Table 20 Economic development in Africa

Oil exploitation in the Niger Delta	Land grabs in West Africa
<ul><li>Oil exports represent about 25% of Nigeria's GDP</li><li>Oil drilling by foreign TNCs in the Niger Delta region has generated conflict with the indigenous Ogoni people over land rights</li><li>Bombings, kidnappings, shootings and mass protests have plagued the region for decades</li><li>Thousands of oil spills, possibly of over 9 million barrels of oil since the 1950s, have caused widespread damage to forests, swamps and human health</li></ul>	<ul><li>So-called 'land grabs' involve foreign TNCs and SWFs buying up farmland in developing countries</li><li>The land is used for cash-crops (coffee, palm oil)</li><li>Subsistence farmers are evicted or paid compensation to leave</li><li>The ability of local people to feed themselves by farming is reduced</li><li>In Senegal, about 12% of arable land is under foreign ownership</li><li>However, about 20% of Senegal's population is under-nourished</li></ul>

Military intervention

There are many examples where Western countries have undertaken military intervention in other sovereign states. The number of sovereign states that do this is small:

- Britain, France and the USA intervene quite regularly either as part of a United Nations intervention, a **NATO** led intervention (Libya in 2011, Bosnia in 1992–95) or unilaterally
- Russia tends to intervene if it perceives a threat directly on its borders (annexation of Crimea from Ukraine in 2014, USSR invasion of Afghanistan in 1979): its military intervention in the Syrian conflict since 2015 is unusual
- other countries provide troops, equipment and financial backing for **UN Peacekeeping forces**, but these are not offensive combat operations
- the terms of the peace treaties at the end of the Second World War limit the ability of Japan and Germany to undertake military intervention

Military interventions are often justified on human rights grounds. In some examples the case for this is strong, but less so in other cases (Table 21). Most interventions are more about wider global strategic interests — in other words military intervention is undertaken to protect the interests of Western powers, such as:

- a need to protect strategic resources, such as oil supply, especially from the Middle East. Intervention in Iraq in the 1990s and 2000s by the USA and its allies can partly be seen in this context

- the need to protect shipping routes for oil, gas and other goods, such as the Suez and Panama canals, the Red Sea and Persian Gulf. If these narrow shipping routes were controlled by hostile countries, there could be large economic consequences
- the need to prevent wider conflict destabilising whole regions: NATO intervention in Bosnia in 1992–95 was partly to prevent the Bosnian War spilling over into other European countries

Table 21 Human rights as a justification for military intervention

NATO intervention in Bosnia 1992–95	2003 Invasion of Iraq	UK intervention in Sierra Leone, 2000
Background In 1995, an attack on Bosnian Muslims by Bosnian Serbs led to 8,000 deaths and became known as the 'Srebrenica Massacre'. This led to the NATO Operation Deliberate Force — an offensive air and bombing campaign against the Bosnian Serbs	**Background** A US- and UK-led invasion that led to the downfall of Iraqi leader Saddam Hussein. It was justified at the time on the basis of removing Iraq's weapons of mass destruction, especially chemical weapons, and Iraq's support for terrorism	**Background** Operation Palliser was a UK unilateral intervention in the Sierra Leone civil war after a failed UN-led operation. UK military forces quickly stabilised Sierra Leone, defeating the Revolutionary United Front (RUF) rebel forces and implementing a ceasefire
Human rights Strong human rights justification, which eventually led to war crimes arrests among Bosnian Serb military leaders	**Human rights** WMD were never found in Iraq by USA and UK forces, and some argue the conflict and its aftermath inflicted greater human rights abuses than existed before the invasion	**Human rights** The RUF committed mass killings, used rape as a weapon of war, and used child soldiers. Ending these atrocities and war crimes provided a strong human rights justification

It is important to recognise that military intervention does not always take place, even when it appears to be strongly justified. Recent examples of **genocide** include:

- Darfur genocide in Sudan (2003–ongoing), with estimates of 100,000–500,000 deaths by 2018
- Rwandan genocide of the Tutsi people by Hutus (1994), estimated to have led to at least 500,000 deaths

In addition, between 2016 and 2018 the government and military of Myanmar have forced about 950,000 Rohingya Muslims to flee the country, mostly to Bangladesh. This is an example of **ethnic cleansing** (although some NGOs have called it genocide). In all of these cases, the UN and NGOs have intervened with emergency aid, awareness raising and, in some cases, peacekeeping forces. However, direct military action to stop the genocide/ethnic cleansing was not taken by Western powers such as the USA, UK or France.

Weapons of mass destruction, or **WMD**, are chemical, biological or nuclear weapons that kill large numbers of people indiscriminately. Many are illegal based on international treaties.

Exam tip

When using examples of conflicts, and interventions in them, make sure you get place names, opposing sides and dates correct in your answers.

Genocide is the deliberate attempt to destroy a people, i.e. a religious or ethnic group, by mass killings.

Ethnic cleansing is the forced removal of an ethnic or religious group from a territory. It is often a precursor to genocide, or occurs alongside genocide.

Military aid

Military aid is an important part of the foreign policy of some developed and emerging countries. It is especially important to the USA, which provides military aid to over 100 countries each year. Figure 7 shows the top ten recipients in 2017. Most aid goes to the Middle East. Iraq, Afghanistan, Israel and Egypt each received over US$1 billion in 2017. The aid is partly used to fight terrorism, and partly to rebuild military and police forces in countries such as Iraq and Afghanistan after years of conflict. However, it has wider geopolitical aims:

- by arming Iraq, Afghanistan, Pakistan and Jordan the USA is creating strong allies against Iran — which the USA sees as a destabilising influence in the Middle East
- the USA supports Israel (an enemy of Iran) partly because the Jewish vote is important in internal US politics, and the USA sees a powerful Israel as an important component of stability in the Middle East
- Egypt controls the Suez Canal, a vital world trade shipping route important to American businesses, so by giving military aid to Egypt the USA may hope to safeguard access to the canal

Military aid takes the form of training another country's military personnel to fight, or operate military equipment, plus the supply of weapons either for free or at subsidised prices.

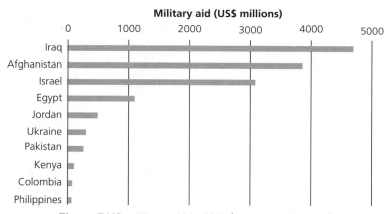

Figure 7 US military aid in 2017 (top ten recipients)

Developed countries sell **arms** to developing and emerging countries. World trade in arms is dominated by exports from six countries (USA, Russia, China, Germany, UK, France). In 2017 the USA exported US$42 billion worth of arms to other countries. The three largest buyers of US weapons are countries which themselves have questionable human rights records:

Arms mean military equipment of all types, from guns and bullets to guided missiles and fighter jets.

1 **Saudi Arabia**: the position of women is very poor in terms of education, personal freedom, political involvement and employment

2 **Turkey**: since 2010 President Erdogan has restricted press and media freedom, and arrested thousands of opposition political leaders and activists: Turkish elections are not a model of democracy

3 **UAE**: stoning and flogging are legal punishments, homosexuality is a crime, women need the permission of a male guardian to marry and the working conditions for hundreds of thousands of South-Asian low-skilled migrant workers are very poor

Both arms sales and military aid flow towards countries which have poor records on human rights. There is an argument that such assistance increases security, reduces the terrorism risk and may even help maintain peace in the Middle East. On the other hand, the billions involved could be put to work improving food and water supply, female education or healthcare for mothers and children.

War on Terror

The phrase 'War on Terror' was first used in 2001 by US President George W. Bush, shortly after the 9/11 attacks on the World Trade Center in New York. The phrase means a war against **Islamic extremism** and the groups that support it, including:

- Al-Qaeda in Afghanistan and Arabia
- the Taliban in Afghanistan
- Boko Haram in Nigeria
- Islamic State (ISIS) in Syria and Iraq
- Al-Shabaab in Somalia

These groups have committed atrocities in their own countries, and claimed responsibility for numerous terrorist attacks in Western countries, such as the 2015 attack on the Bataclan Theatre in Paris and the 2017 attack on Westminster Bridge in London.

Western countries, led by the USA but often involving the UK, France and others, have justified direct military intervention in a number of countries because of the War on Terror, including:

- **drone** strikes in Pakistan, Afghanistan, Yemen, Somalia and other places
- the 2003 invasion of Iraq
- conflict in Afghanistan from 2001 and continuing as of 2018
- air strikes and special forces operations in Syria and Iraq, against Islamic State

There have also been US-led operations in the Philippines, Mali and elsewhere in Africa. In 2014, Western countries used airstrikes, fooddrops and military support for Kurdish forces to attempt to prevent the massacre of the Yazidi ethno-religious minority group by ISIS in Sinjar, Iraq. To some extent, French military intervention in Mali since 2013 has been to protect minority groups such as the Malian Sufis from Islamic extremists.

The War on Terror raises several difficult questions related to the UN UDHR.

1 To what extent do people in Muslim countries want their human rights protected by Western countries?
   - In 1990, 48 Muslim countries signed the Cairo Declaration on Human Rights in Islam. The CDHRI is a response to criticism that the UDHR fails to take account of the Islamic perspective on human rights or the role of Sharia law. In other words, justification for intervention based on the UDHR may have limited support in some Muslim countries.

2 To what extent are the actions of Western countries undermined by their own attitude towards the UDHR?
   - The USA has been accused of using torture at secret CIA 'black sites' around the world, and both US and UK forces were accused of illegal use of torture during the 2003 Iraq war. Many Western countries have patchy records on human rights protection for their indigenous groups.

Knowledge check 18

Which country is the largest supplier of arms to other countries, and the largest supplier of military aid?

Islamic extremism — sometimes called Islamism or Islamic fundamentalism — is a radical form of Islam seeking to remove or destroy non-Islamic influences and religions from society, and create Islamic religious states under Sharia law.

A **drone** is an unmanned aircraft, capable of carrying out a missile strike without risking the life of a pilot. They often operate unseen and undetected and are controlled from bases thousands of miles away.

Exam tip

Think carefully about the language and terminology you use when writing about the War on Terror. Keep it factual and balanced and avoid sweeping generalisations.

3 To what extent does the War on Terror risk a permanent cultural divide?
- The War on Terror may risk demonising all Muslims, not just Islamists, and therefore create mistrust within Western countries (many of which have large Muslim minorities) and between Western and Muslim countries.

What are the outcomes of geopolitical interventions in terms of human development and human rights?

- The success of geopolitical interventions can be measured in different ways, focusing on economic development or measures of freedom, democracy or equality.
- The role of development aid in terms of improving human rights and human wellbeing is contested and its track record of success is mixed.
- Both direct and indirect military interventions have been successful, but in other cases there have been long-term costs.

Measuring success

Interventions in sovereign states — whether humanitarian, military or the use of development aid — should improve the lives of people in a measurable way. There is no universally accepted way of measuring the 'success' of interventions. Table 22 evaluates a number of commonly used measures.

Table 22 Measuring the success of interventions

Measure	Advantages	Disadvantages
Infant mortality (deaths before age 1, per 1,000 live births)	■ Responds rapidly to changes in sanitation and access to basic health and nutrition ■ Correlates strongly with the quality of governance in a state	■ Recording is often poor in isolated rural areas ■ Improvements in health systems sometimes lead to an increase in recorded infant mortality
Life expectancy (average life years from birth)	■ Widely understood, comparable measure ■ Relatively easy to calculate from existing records	■ Responds relatively slowly to improving social conditions ■ National average masks wide regional, local and ethnicity variations
Net primary enrolment (% of primary-school-aged children, in school)	■ Increases suggest rising literacy, and falling child labour use ■ Relatively easy to calculate	■ Does not indicate female versus male enrolment, i.e. gender equality ■ Only indicates education up to age 10–11
GDP per capita (average income per person)	■ Widely used, easy-to-understand measure of average wealth ■ Simple to calculate, and update	■ Does not indicate income distribution or income equality ■ Does not take into account the cost of living

Single indicators, such as those shown in Table 22, can indicate success but an **index** is often a better method such as the:

- Human Development Index (HDI): combining per capita income, life expectancy and average years in school
- Gender Inequality Index (GII): combining maternal mortality, women's participation in higher education and parliament, and participation in the workforce

An **index** combines a number of single measures of human and economic development into one measure: this increases data range, and reduces the impact of anomalous single measures.

Improvements in these indices show relatively widespread progress in human wellbeing, the position of women and human rights. Freedom of speech, as included in the UDHR, is measured using indices such as the Reporters Without Borders 'Press Freedom Index' or the EIU Democracy Index.

Many interventions involve the management of refugees fleeing conflict either internally or internationally. The extent to which refugees are treated humanely is important. They should be:

- provided with shelter, food, water and healthcare
- reunited with other family members
- in time, supported to return to their homes or permanently resettled as asylum seekers

Surprisingly, Uganda is a model of refugee management. In 2018 there were around 600,000 refugees and asylum seekers in Uganda from 13 other African countries. Many are from South Sudan, Somalia and the DRC. Uganda's progressive legal system:

- allows refugees to work, to support their families
- gives them access to social services such as healthcare and education
- allows freedom of movement within Uganda
- in many cases provides refugee families with land to farm

These policies contrast starkly with those in many Western countries, such as the UK, which prohibit some of these freedoms.

Democracy as 'success'

Western governments, especially the USA (and to a lesser extent EU countries and IGOs such as the UN) see the promotion of democracy and **freedom of expression** as a key outcome of intervention.

Most countries that carry out interventions are Western, capitalist democracies. It is perhaps not surprising that these countries equate freedom and democracy with 'success'. However, as Figure 8 shows, few countries score highly on the Cato Institute's Human Freedom Index. In fact less than 40% of the world's population live in countries that are 'free'. Freedom and democracy is less common than might be expected:

- there is very little tradition of freedom, democratic elections or gender equality in the Middle East
- 60 years ago, most African countries were colonies: democracy has struggled to take root there

Western countries could be criticised for forcing their own economic and political model on developing and emerging countries, when 'success' might actually be measured in terms of rising incomes, improving life expectancy and increasing participation in education. Interestingly, in a 2015 survey by Pew Global Research only 53% of people in Pakistan and 52% in Turkey agreed with the statement 'Do you think people should be able to criticise the government's policies?' In the USA and UK, the figures were 95% and 94%. Support for complete freedom of speech is not universal.

Knowledge check 19

Which index combines measures of income, education and life expectancy?

Exam tip

Single indicator or index data are often used as stimulus material in the exam paper, so make sure you are familiar with them, and the units used.

Freedom of expression is the principle that individuals and communities have the right to articulate their opinions and ideas without fear of retaliation, censorship or sanction. It is part of the UDHR.

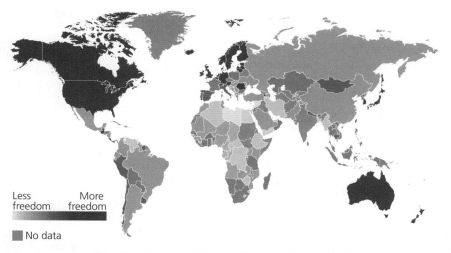

The Cato Institute, Human Freedom Index 2017

Figure 8 The Human Freedom Index

Economic growth as 'success'

In some countries the success of foreign aid, military interventions to end conflict and trade embargoes or sanctions is measured by subsequent economic growth rather than an improvement in human rights or a growth of democracy. The concept of **holistic development** (Figure 9), where many aspects of human wellbeing are improved at the same time, is seen as less important than improving wealth and incomes.

In some ways this makes sense.

- In developed countries democracy and human rights are relatively new, having developed only in the last 200 years: they were largely absent as today's developed countries industrialised and became wealthy.

- In developing countries without government-funded welfare systems people have to pay for education, healthcare and clean water: rising incomes make this possible far more than the right to vote.

- Families in developing countries often have to look after elderly relatives, and income is needed for this when there are no government pensions.

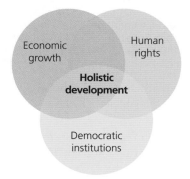

Figure 9 Holistic development

Knowledge check 20

On Figure 8, which global regions appear to be least 'free'?

Holistic development means progress in incomes, education, equality, health, housing, human rights and freedom; in other words, all aspects of quality of life not just one or two aspects.

On the other hand, ignoring the need for human rights and democratic institutions as part of the development process risks authoritarian rule, poor governance and corruption, and possibly even persecution of minority groups. There are examples of countries that have transitioned to democracy as they have developed economically such as Taiwan (1996), South Korea (1987), Indonesia (1999) and Ecuador (1979) which suggests that growing wealth can promote democracy and freedom.

The successes and failures of aid

Development aid and intervention have a very mixed track record of success. In theory, intervention and aid promoted by Western countries should promote economic and social development, improve health and education and increase human rights. The examples in Table 23 show this is not always the case.

Table 23 Examples of intervention

Country	Details	Evaluation
Ebola crisis (2013–16) in Guinea, Sierra Leone and Liberia	■ Epidemic that killed over 11,000 people ■ Reduced GDP by 10–15% in the affected countries ■ The World Health Organization, the UK, the USA and France led the international response	After a slow initial response the epidemic was contained, but at a cost of over US$4 billion Without international intervention Ebola could have spread in an uncontrolled way with even worse consequences
Botswana (since independence in 1966)	■ Africa's fastest growing and most democratic country ■ 62% of its exports are diamonds ■ Tourism contributes 12% of GDP ■ It has received much foreign investment by TNCs in mining, tourism and finance	Democracy and lack of corruption have promoted foreign investment 25% of the population are HIV positive, but for 20 years a sound education and health programme have attempted to control **AIDS/HIV** with some success
Haiti	■ USA invasion and occupation 1915–34 ■ 1957–86 Haiti was ruled by father and son dictators Francois and Jean-Claude Duvalier, tolerated by the USA ■ US military intervention 1994–95 to reinstate President Aristide ■ 2004 onwards: UN intervention to stabilise Haiti's political situation	The poorest country in the western hemisphere has been badly governed and subject to foreign intervention for over 100 years. It was ill-prepared for the devastating 2010 earthquake and subsequent cholera epidemic
Iraq	■ 1990–91 invasion of southern Iraq by US-led forces after retaking Kuwait, which Iraq had invaded ■ 2003 invasion by a US-led Western coalition to overthrow President Saddam Hussein ended in 2011 ■ Since 2014 there has been a civil war in Iraq	Military intervention freed Kuwait, and eventually removed the dictator Saddam Hussein. However, Iraq has since been a fragmented country divided by religious and ethnic conflict

Ebola is a deadly virus present in Africa, which has periodic outbreaks and epidemics. It has a mortality rate of around 70% and it is both very hard to treat and to control its spread.

The **HIV** virus is a disease most often spread by sexual activity, which can develop into **AIDS**. AIDS can be treated, but this is costly and there is no cure. It is most common in the countries of southern and East Africa.

Exam tip

'Development' is quite a contested term: it can be interpreted in a narrow economic way, or a much broader way. Make sure you read exam questions carefully to understand what type of 'development' is being referred to.

Knowledge check 21

Which Western countries led the intervention to control the Ebola epidemic in West Africa?

Aid and equality

Development aid, often combined with intervention that attempts to manage epidemics, natural disasters or conflict, should reduce **economic inequality** and improve people's lives. Figure 10 shows how the Human Development Index (HDI) changed between 1990 and 2015 for four countries:

- Haiti's improvement is small and slow: the 2010 earthquake halted progress briefly.
- Ghana's HDI increased significantly after 2000: this is partly due to increased development aid flowing to Ghana within the UN Millennium Development Goal framework. Since 2004 Ghana has received US$1.1–1.8 billion in aid each year.
- Vietnam has made the fastest, steadiest progress: this is a result of up to US$4 billion in aid annually, but perhaps more the result of foreign investment by TNCs as Vietnam globalises and copies the Chinese model of manufacturing exports.
- Iraq, subject to huge foreign military intervention since 1990 and over US$50 billion of aid between 2004 and 2008, has made the least HDI progress. Since 2012, HDI trends have reversed because of ongoing civil war.

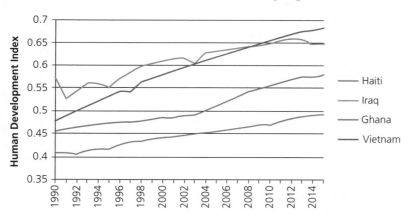

Figure 10 HDI trends 1990–2015

All four countries in Figure 10 have reported increased life expectancy since 1990 (Table 24). Iraq has had the least progress — a result of conflict, invasions, terrorism and the brutal rule of Saddam Hussein prior to 2003. Perhaps suprisingly, Haiti has made the most progress. However, this was from the lowest starting point: aid has improved health outcomes but this has often not translated into wider social and economic opportunities. Table 25 shows that both Haiti and Ghana have very unequal income distributions, with close to 50% of each country's wealth in the hands of the richest 20%. This suggests that development progress may be benefiting the wealthy more than the poor. In Vietnam, income inequality is lower, perhaps because the low-skilled jobs that globalisation has created are accessible to the poor.

Table 24 Life expectancy 1990–2015

	1990	2015	Percentage change
Haiti	54.6	63.1	+ 16%
Iraq	66.2	69.6	+ 5%
Ghana	56.8	61.5	+ 8%
Vietnam	70.5	75.9	+ 8%

Economic inequality refers to how fairly or equally income is distributed in a country or region. It is often measured using the Gini Coefficient. This quantifies the share of national income (GDP) going to different quintiles (fifths) of the population, e.g. the poorest 20%, or richest 20%.

Exam tip

You need to know examples of interventions, including dates, names and facts: accurate evidence is important in essay questions.

Knowledge check 22

On Figure 10, which is the only country with recorded sustained declines in HDI since 1990?

Table 25 Income inequality in 2015

Country	Percentage share of GDP going to:	
	Poorest 20% of people	Richest 20% of people
Ghana	5.4	48.8
Haiti	5.5	47.1
Iraq	8.8	38.5
Vietnam	7.1	42.2

Aid as foreign policy

A major issue with development aid is the suspicion that it often has as much to do with geopolitics as it does with improving socio-economic conditions in developing countries. This is especially true of bilateral aid given from one country to another (Figure 11). Aid can be used by superpowers to assist geostrategic interests.

- Chinese aid to Pakistan, Sri Lanka, Russia and Turkmenistan is linked to the Chinese One Belt One Road economic plan, sometimes called the 'New Silk Road'. This is a massive plan to develop new sea and land trade routes between China, South Asia, the Middle East and Europe.
- French and UK aid is funnelled towards former colonies: English-speaking East Africa (Commonwealth countries) and Francophone West Africa which helps maintain old alliances.
- French aid is perhaps the most global, as France seeks strategic partners worldwide.
- UK and US aid often overlap, especially in the Middle East and East Africa where Islamic terrorism is viewed as a threat that must be countered.

Aid can lubricate a number of wider interests including:

- opening up access to natural resources such as oil, metal ores and minerals: often cited as a key reason behind Chinese aid to African nations
- strengthening military alliances: this is one reason why France gives aid to Turkey as both are members of NATO and why USA and UK aid often goes to the same countries because the UK and USA are military allies
- USA aid to Ukraine strengthens the alliance between those countries against Russia (which invaded and annexed Crimea from Ukraine in 2014)

Although very hard to specifically prove, aid recipients might be expected to support their donor countries within IGOs such as the United Nations or WTO, i.e. aid can help win political support.

Military interventions

There have been many direct and indirect military interventions in recent history. UN peacekeepers have been involved in the Democratic Republic of Congo (DRC) since 1999, intervening in the Second Congo War. The war is a fight between DRC government forces under President Laurent Kabila and various rebel groups under the RCD (Rally for Congolese Democracy) flag. At stake is control of the DRC and its vast mineral wealth — including **conflict minerals** such as gold, diamonds and coltan (used in mobile phones). It has an ethnic dimension, and has spilled over into Uganda, Rwanda and Burundi.

Conflict minerals are high-value minerals and ores, such as gold and diamonds, that have caused war as opposing groups fight to control mining and trade.

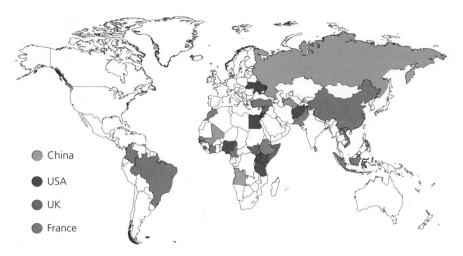

Figure 11 Top ten recipients of aid from France, China, the UK and USA, 2016–17

Legend:
- China
- USA
- UK
- France

Knowledge check 23

Which types of countries do France and the UK often give development aid to?

Exam tip

Make sure you are clear that development aid is controversial and frequently has multiple aims, i.e. humanitarian as well as political.

- In 2017 there were 18,300 UN peacekeepers in the DRC operating as MONUSCO (United Nations Organization Stabilization Mission in the Democratic Republic of the Congo).
- More than 30 member states have contributed troops.
- The total cost has been over US$9 billion.

Table 26 considers the gains and costs of the UN action.

Table 26 Evaluating UN Peacekeeping in the DRC

Gains	Costs
■ The situation may have been worse without UN involvement ■ The UN may have prevented wider, direct involvement by other countries, i.e. an African World War ■ The UN has collected evidence that may lead to war crimes trials ■ Humanitarian help and aid has been provided by the UN, protected by peacekeepers	■ Despite 20 years of UN action, the war still raged in Ituri and Kivu regions in 2018 ■ DRC is more dependent than ever on warlord-controlled conflict minerals ■ Over 5 million dead, including 200 UN peacekeepers ■ Income in DRC is about US$400 per person per year ■ Shocking war crimes, involving child soldiers and sexual violence, have been widespread

Sometimes individual nation states act on their own. An example is the UK's intervention in Sierra Leone (a former UK colony) in 2000, considered to be a **failed state** at that time.

- Sierra Leone descended into civil war in 1991, and by 1999 more than 50,000 were dead.
- The UN became involved in 1999, but this intervention failed and the UK decided to step in.
- Operation Palliser, with 1,200 troops, naval and air support, drove rebel forces back from Freetown, the capital city, and led to a ceasefire.
- UK intervention saved the UN mission in Sierra Leone.

A **failed state** is a nation state where governance has broken down and there is no effective state that can protect the nation of people. Basic services (water, health) have collapsed and the lack of security risks people's lives on a daily basis.

By 2002, the war was over and the country has made progress since. Several war criminals were prosecuted, including Charles Taylor (rebel leader), convicted of war crimes in 2012. The UK's intervention is viewed as having been highly successful. Table 27 summarises some other recent military interventions.

France intervened in the 2011 Second Ivorian Civil War, in order to end a brutal conflict between military supporters of Alassane Ouattara (the democratically elected president) and Laurent Gbagbo (loser of the 2010 presidential election). French special forces helped arrest Gbagbo and restore Ouattara to power. Subsequently Côte d'Ivoire has been relatively stable and Ouattara was re-elected president in 2015.

Table 27 Examples of interventions

The USA's 'War on Terror' since 2001	UK and France in Libya, 2011
Military actions around the world against Islamic terrorists (Al Qaeda, Taliban, Islamic State) in response to the 9/11 attacks on the World Trade Center in New York	An air force bombing campaign in support of rebel forces fighting the government forces of Colonel Gaddafi. In the context of the 2011 Arab Spring
■ Viewed as 'demonising' the Muslim religion ■ Turned some Muslims in Western countries into radical Islamists ■ Contributed to the rise of Islamic State — as an extremist response to the 'War on Terror' ■ Made Middle Eastern countries 'take sides', i.e. for or against the USA	■ Disagreement among NATO members over how to act ■ Disintegration of governance in Libya ■ Refugee and humanitarian crisis in Libya as no effective government has emerged since 2011 ■ Widespread disregard for human rights

Any military intervention, either by the UN, a coalition of countries or an individual country inevitably means the sovereignty of the country where the intervention takes place is severely eroded. This means the 'bar' for intervention is high.

In some cases intervention may make a bad human rights situation worse. Failed intervention risks prolonging conflict, with greater numbers of deaths, injuries and human rights abuses. The West's failure to create a situation where a stable, unified, democractic post-intervention government could exist in Somalia, Libya, Iraq or Afghanistan begs the very difficult question as to whether those countries would have been better off without Western intervention.

The consequences of inaction

It is possible to argue that military intervention can be positive, despite the risks. In a 2007 book, Professor Paul Collier (Director of Oxford's Centre for the Study of African Economies) argued that the cost of a nation becoming a 'failed state' was US$30 billion and recovery back to a 'normal' state took 59 years on average. In other words, the long-term costs to human wellbeing and human rights are probably worse than the short-term costs of intervening.

The costs of the Syrian Civil War that began in 2011 have been huge:
■ between 350,000 and 500,000 deaths up to 2018
■ 7.6 million people internally displaced within Syria
■ 5.1 million international refugees
■ a refugee crisis, which has caused internal political division within the EU

Exam tip

You are not expected to be a historian, but inaccurate details about examples of conflict (dates, death tolls, costs) will undermine your answers so some detailed learning is inevitable.

The **Arab Spring** in 2011 was a popular uprising against military dictatorships in North Africa (Libya, Tunisia, Egypt) and the Middle East (Syria, Iran) which led to the overthrow of several governments but also longer-term conflict in Syria and Libya.

Knowledge check 24

What is the estimated cost of the UN intervention in the Democractic Republic of Congo up to 2017?

- the rise of Islamic State (ISIS) within Syria and beyond
- tensions between Russia, Turkey, the EU and USA in terms of how to respond
- the use of chemical weapons by President Assad's forces
- widespread destruction of ancient, globally significant heritage sites such as Aleppo and Palmyra
- environmental pollution caused by destroyed water and sewage systems, and chemical contamination from weapons, destroyed factories and military equipment

While the West has intervened in terms of air strikes and missile strikes against ISIS, and Turkey and Russia (pro-Syrian government) have also been involved militarily, there has not been a 'boots on the ground' intervention by the West as there was in Iraq or Afghanistan. Could this have shortened the civil war?

The long-term impact on Syrians is considerable:

- by 2018, the Syrian economy was about 40% of its size in 2010
- unemployment has risen to over 50%, whereas GDP per capita has collapsed by 50%
- HDI has fallen from 0.65 in 2010, to around 0.5 by 2018

President Assad estimated in 2017 that post-war reconstruction costs, once the war ends, would be US$400 billion (eight times the estimated annual GDP of Syria in 2018).

Summary

- Development can be measured in quite a narrow, economic way but in the last few decades it has become common to consider wider human wellbeing, environmental quality, education and human rights as part of 'development'.
- Health and life expectancy vary both within countries and between countries. The causes of variations are complex and include poverty as well as ethnicity and lifestyle.
- Different governments, IGOs, NGOs and others prioritise different aspects of development — such as economic growth, human rights, equality or free trade. Globally the 2000–15 MDGs and post-2015 SDGs are important development frameworks.
- Human rights are often considered to be universal, and are enshrined in international, EU and UK law — but not everyone agrees on the definition or universality of human rights.
- Freedom, democracy, levels of corruption and freedom of speech vary widely around the world and this has a significant impact on human rights reflected in differences between genders, ethnicities and minority groups.
- Interventions by IGOs, NGOs and national governments can be justified on human rights grounds and take the form of direct and indirect military action, trade embargoes and sanctions and the use of development aid.
- Development aid is controversial because it can increase dependency or can be used as a political tool. However it can promote development progress, Human rights and human wellbeing.
- Military interventions and military aid are used to protect human rights but this has a mixed record of success.
- The success of interventions can be measured in a multitude of different ways including single and composite development measures, the spread of democracy and economic development: different players focus on different measures of success.

■ Migration, identity and sovereignty

What are the impacts of globalisation on international migration?

- Globalisation is strongly linked to migration: globalisation has accelerated migration both within and between countries.
- There are different types of migrants and motivations for migrating, but the ease at which people can move from place to place varies.
- Migration leads to cultural change, and political tensions: its costs and benefits are disputed and there are variations in policies towards immigrants.

Globalisation and migration

Migrants are people who move from one location (a source area) to a new location (a destination) permanently. 'Permanent' is usually defined as for a year or more. Migration can be:

- **internal**: within a country, e.g. from the north of England to London
- **external**: between countries, e.g. a UK citizen migrating to Germany

Figure 12 shows how the stock of international migrants has grown since 1990. If all international migrants were a country, it would be the world's fifth most populous. International migration has accelerated since the year 2000, and **globalisation** has played a key role in this.

Since 1980, globalisation has changed the global economic system. The **global shift** has created new locations of economic growth and job creation — and job losses elsewhere. These economic changes have driven changes in migration, because demand for labour (workers) has changed. Table 28 gives some examples of the global shift and migration link.

Globalisation is the economic process that has created wider, faster and deeper connections between places and contributed to the idea of a 'shrinking world'.

The **global shift** is the movement of jobs from developed countries such as the UK and USA, to new locations in emerging economies such as China and Mexico. It has affected both manufacturing and services.

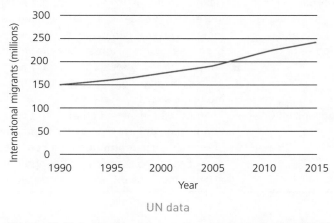

UN data

Figure 12 Global stock of international migrants, 1990–2015

Knowledge check 25

Look at Figure 12. What was the increase in the global migrant stock between 1990 and 2015?

Table 28 Migration and the global shift

Location	Global shift	Impact on migration
Pearl River Delta, China	Outsourcing of manufacturing jobs by developed world TNCs to lower-cost locations	Mass internal **rural–urban migration** from the countryside to China's cities, especially of men and women aged 15–25
UAE, Qatar and Bahrain	Growth of the small Gulf States as an air travel, finance and tourism hub situated between Europe and Asia	International elite migration of professional workers from the developed world, plus large-scale low-skill migration from South Asia (construction workers, domestic servants)
The USA Rustbelt	Deindustrialisation in old industrial revolution heartlands of the developed world, caused by factory closures	Internal migration from the northeast Rustbelt (Detroit, Pittsburg, Buffalo) to the southwest Sunbelt (California, Arizona), as people move to find work
Bangalore, Chennai and Pune in India	Offshoring of call-centre and back-office functions, by developed-world TNCs, to low-cost locations, utilising internet and mobile phone networks	Internal rural–urban migration from the Indian countryside to cities, especially of graduates

International migration within EU countries has increased because:

- in 1990, there were 12 EU member states, increasing to 28 by 2013
- a key EU principle is freedom of movement of workers between all member states
- since 1993, the EU has operated the Single Market: a **free-trade area** for goods and services, promoting labour migration
- many EU and other European countries have joined the passport-free Schengen Area since 1995, making migration across borders easier than ever

Variations in migration

Globally, 3.3% of the population live outside their home country. There is large variation between countries and regions. In sub-Saharan Africa the percentage of immigrants is 2%, whereas in Europe it is 10%. There are reasons for variations in immigrant population (Figure 13).

- Some countries, such as the UAE, Qatar and Singapore are global hubs for trade, transport and tourism. These highly globalised places attract many types of migrants, and have flexible immigration and visa policies to help promote economic growth.
- Canada, Australia and the USA actively encouraged immigration for much of the twentieth century to populate their young, vast countries.
- EU countries all conform to the policies of the Single Market and free movement, encouraging migration.
- Emerging countries (South Africa, Malaysia, Turkey) are engaging with the global economy as they grow, encouraging immigration.
- Developing countries are less globalised: people migrate internally to cities but lack the means and skills to consider international migration.

Some countries are exceptions. Only 1.6% of Japan's population are immigrants, much lower than other developed countries. The reasons for this are complex.

Rural–urban migration involves people, usually young, moving from their traditional homes in the countryside to towns and cities in search of work.

A **free-trade area** is the result of a trade agreement removing tariffs, taxes and quotas on imports and exports so goods (and sometimes services) can move barrier-free across international borders.

Exam tip

You have covered Globalisation in Topic 3, so it would be useful to review that work as you revise this topic.

- Japan's immigration policies are not particularly strict towards economic migrants (they are strict towards refugees), it is rather that fewer people than might be expected apply to migrate to Japan.
- The Japanese language and homogenous culture may make integrating into Japanese society harder than in Europe or North America.
- In many developed countries there are already thriving immigrant communities that newcomers can be part of, but this is not the case in Japan.
- Immigrants to the USA often become 'American' in terms of culture and attitudes after a short period of time; in Japan the sense of being 'foreign' tends to remain.

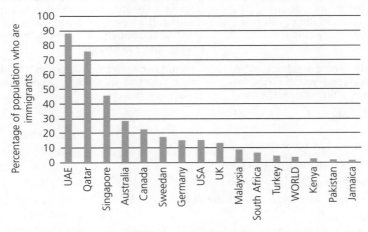

Figure 13 Variations in immigrant population

There is a difference between being an immigrant and holding **citizenship**. Many immigrants move to new countries using long-term work or residency **visas**. Becoming a legal citizen can be very hard. The UAE's population is almost 90% foreign, but almost none of these immigrants will become Emirati citizens because citizenship rules are very strict. They are less strict in many countries, but usually require living in a country for a long period, taking a 'citizenship test', e.g. in the UK and USA, and in some cases giving up previous citizenship.

Changing migration

Most of the world's international migrants are voluntary economic ones. People have chosen to migrate to look for better economic opportunities. The vast majority are legal immigrants: they have visas, work permits and other documents that allow them to work in a new country. There are other types of migrant:

- **refugees**: migrants forced to move across an international border to escape a threat (war, political persecution, genocide, famine or the impacts of natural disasters)
- **asylum seekers**: these are refugees who have applied for asylum, i.e. the right to remain in another country, and are awaiting a decision
- **illegal immigrants**: those who have entered a foreign country without documentation, but have done so voluntarily
- **trafficked illegal migrants**: people forced, or tricked, into migrating to a country who often end up as sex workers, or in modern slavery

Knowledge check 26

What percentage of the world's population are immigrants?

Citizenship means being a legal member of a sovereign state (country) with the rights that this brings, such as the right to vote, and live and work indefinitely in that sovereign state.

A **visa** is a legal document allowing a person to enter a foreign country. Visas have conditions setting out how long people can stay and whether or not they can work.

Exam tip

Make sure you know the terminology for different types of migrant, especially terms such as 'refugee' or 'asylum seeker' as they are easy to confuse.

The number of illegal and trafficked immigrants is not known because these migrants hide from authority. Home Office and London School of Economic estimates from the mid-2000s ranged from 300,000 to 800,000 in the UK. Table 29 shows some of the largest **net migration** flows, 2010–15.

> **Net migration** is the difference between outflows or losses (emigration) and inflows or gains (immigration) over a period of time.

Table 29 Largest net migration flows, 2010–15

Net emigration		Net immigration	
Syria −4,685,000	Forced migration of refugees fleeing the civil war since 2011	USA +3,063,000	Economic migrants, often highly skilled, seeking better opportunities
India −2,470,000 Pakistan −1,223,000	Low-skilled economic migration to the UAE, Oman, Qatar and Kuwait	UK +547,000	Migration from other EU member states, plus former Commonwealth countries
		Turkey +1,434,000	Inflow from the Syria conflict
Philippines −652,000	Domestic servants, maids and nurses moving to developed and emerging countries	UAE +896,000	Inflow from South Asian countries (low skilled) plus elite workers from developed countries
Sudan −765,000	Movement of people from Sudan to the new country of South Sudan following the 2011 split of Sudan into two countries	South Africa +714,000	Largely male, manual workers from nearby southern African countries to work in the mining industry

Migration flows do change over time:

- the political conflict in Syria since 2011 has led to a refugee crisis, displacing over 4 million people over international borders and perhaps 6 million internally
- Twenty years ago, migration flows to the UAE, Qatar and Oman were tiny, but economic growth has created a flow of low-skilled, male workers from South Asia to meet the needs of economic growth
- there is evidence that environmental issues (desertification, unreliable rainfall) in the Sahel is leading to increased migration to the coast of West Africa and its cities, as well as illegal immigration to Europe

Causes of migration

There are many causes of migration. German government statistics from 2017 showed that 22.5% of Germany's population had a migrant background, i.e. were first- or **second-generation** migrants. Table 30 explains the reasons for Germany's largest migrant groups.

> **Knowledge check 27**
>
> Approximately how many refugees, internal and external, have been created by the war in Syria since 2011?

> **Second-generation** migrants are the children of immigrants (the first generation).

Table 30 The origins of Germany's largest migrant groups

600,000 Syrians, 167,000 Vietnamese, 158,000 Bosnians	3,500,000 Russians
Germany has accepted refugees including from the Vietnam War in the 1970s, the Bosnian conflict in the 1990s and recently the civil war in Syria	Many Russians migrated to Germany immediately after the USSR collapsed in 1991 at the end of the Cold War. This was partly driven by poverty as industry and the economy crumbled
2,800,000 Turks	**350,000 Dutch**
From the 1950s to the 1970s large numbers of Turkish people migrated to Germany as part of the *Gastarbeiter* (guest worker) programme, to fill labour shortages in Germany	EU freedom of movement means that the Dutch — and any other EU nationals — can freely live and work in Germany, encouraging cross-border migration

In Germany, and other countries, many first-generation economic immigrants are male and relatively young, aged 18–30. If these migrants are economically successful and settle, they are often later joined by other family members, i.e. wives and children, or wider family. This secondary migration is called family reunification migration: some countries have immigration rules that are less strict for family members than for other immigrants. In the USA it is the most common legal basis for newly arrived immigrants today.

Knowledge check 28

What percentage of Germany's population had a migrant background in 2017?

Since 2014–15, increasing numbers of immigrants have arrived in Europe by crossing the Mediterranean Sea from North Africa and the Near East — sometimes referred to as the 'European migrant crisis'. Over 1 million people made the dangerous crossing in 2015, with thousands drowning as ill-equipped boats sank. Figure 14 shows the nationality of those arriving in Greece and Italy in 2015.

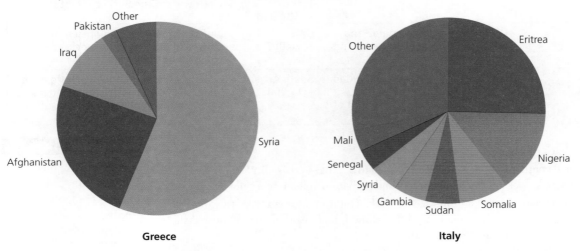

Figure 14 Nationality of immigrants arriving by sea in Greece (left) and Italy (right) 2015 (UNHCR data)

- Most immigrants are refugees from conflicts in Syria, Iraq, Afghanistan and other countries.
- Many immigrants have claimed asylum, and have been granted it.
- Some immigrants are likely to be illegal economic migrants trying to escape poverty in sub-Saharan Africa.

Once in Europe, immigrants can move relatively easily between most EU countries because of the Schengen Area's open borders. Keeping track of this migrant flow is very difficult. Many immigrants arrive with no identification documents, and determining their status is a major challenge. The flow across the Mediterranean slowed in 2017–18 but it still continues.

Migration, identity and sovereignty

Economists argue that migration is good for a country's economy. This is because, from the point of view of **capitalist** economies, economic efficiency (maximum employment, sales and profits) is highest when migration can fill any labour shortages. Migration might be seen as one of the key components of a capitalist economy (Table 31).

Exam tip

As with all topics, it is useful to learn some data on migrant numbers to use as evidence in longer answers.

Capitalism is the world's dominant economic system: it stresses private ownership of businesses, the profit motive, competition between businesses and freedom to trade goods and services.

Table 31 Components of capitalist efficiency

Free trade	Open borders	Deregulated financial markets
International trade in goods and services free from import and export taxes, tariffs and quotas	Labour can move freely to where it is needed by businesses, even across international borders	Banks are free to lend money, and businesses to borrow it, to invest in new economic opportunities

There are reasons to believe international migration is economically beneficial to receiving countries:

■ migrants fill labour shortages, and are often more skilled and better educated than the population as a whole

■ immigrants contribute more in taxes than they receive in social security benefits

■ immigration increases the working age population

■ migrants may be more entrepreneurial and risk-taking

However, open-border immigration may pose a challenge to national sovereignty. Within the EU, freedom of movement means that a citizen of any EU country can move to any other EU country to live and/or work. In the 2016 UK 'Brexit' Referendum those on the 'leave' side of the debate argued that EU freedom of movement meant a loss of UK sovereignty as the UK could not control the numbers of EU immigrants moving to the UK. If fact, the EU is almost the only group of countries in the world that allows freedom of movement of people

Freedom of movement has also accused of challenging **national identity**:

■ host populations feeling 'swamped' by immigrants with different cultural traditions to their own

■ the feeling that immigrants get 'something for nothing', i.e. healthcare without having paid National Insurance

■ physcial changes taking place, especially in cities, where people feel the identity of a place 'feels foreign' because of new immigrant businesses, places of worship and signs in foreign languages

Feelings of loss of sovereignty and erosion of national identity are exceptionally difficult to quantify and measure. However, across the developed world since 2010 numerous national votes have suggested unease with large-scale immigration and other forces such as globalisation (Table 32).

Table 32 Nationalism in elections

52% of people voting in favour of the UK leaving the EU in the 2016 Referendum	Donald Trump's victory in the US general election in 2016, where immigration was a key issue
The Front Nationale (anti-immigration party) gaining 25% of the vote in the 2014 EU election in France, and 34% of the vote in the 2017 presidential election	Alternative für Deutschland (anti-immigration party) winning 13% of the vote in the 2017 German federal elections

National identity is a sense of belonging to a country, based on widely held beliefs, traditions, shared history and shared national symbols.

Exam tip

Immigration is an emotive topic, which is hard to write about in a balanced way. Take care with the language you use in your answers, and always try to provide both sides of the argument before coming to a conclusion.

Labour movement

While there is controversy over freedom of movement in the EU, and international migration more generally, there is much wider acceptance of internal migration between regions of the same country. Figure 15 shows net migration between US states.

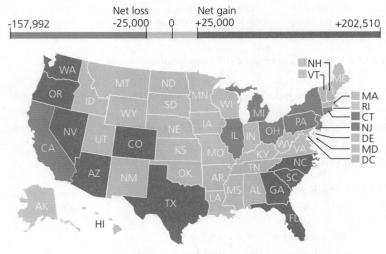

William H. Frey analysis of Census estimates

Figure 15 Net migration between US states, 2014–15

- Southeastern states, including Florida, are major gainers of internal migrants, along with states in the Southwest and Northwest.
- The Northeast is a major loser, especially New York, Michigan, Pennsylvania and Ohio.

The pattern is explained by economic opportunity and lifestyles: many retirees move to Florida and Texas for the year-round warm climate in the so-called 'sunbelt'. Washington State, Colorado and Arizona are areas of economic growth (Amazon and Starbucks are both headquartered in Washington State). The Northeast is the deindustrialised old manufacturing heartland of the USA (the 'Rustbelt') and has experienced mass job losses since the 1970s. California is an anomaly: despite losing internal migrants, its population is still growing because of international migration.

Internal migration has costs and benefits.

- In the UK, London and the southeast are major gainers, but this contributes to congestion, rising house prices and low housing affordability — but a booming economy and youthful population.
- Conversely, net losers — the northeast of England, Wales and Scotland — have ageing populations, a 'brain-drain' of young skilled workers and higher than average levels of people with ill-health.

The EU is unusual in allowing free movement of people across international borders. In most parts of the world international migration is restricted and often only allowed on a temporary basis. There are notable exceptions. As Table 33 shows, the **global elite** can buy the right to live (residency) or become a citizen of many countries.

Knowledge check 29

Which areas of the USA have gained the most internal migrants?

The **global elite** are wealthy individuals with large assets, representing the richest 1% of the world's people.

Table 33 The cost of residency or citizenship in selected countries, 2018

Thailand	Elite Residency for 20 years	$60,000
Latvia	Residency	$350,000
Saint Lucia	Citizenship	$100,000
USA	Residency	$500,000
Canada	Citizenship	$800,000

Assimilation

A potential cost of immigration relates to the degree to which immigrants assimilate into the **host culture**. Over time the process of cultural assimilation means that immigrants:

- adopt the language of the host
- adopt some of the traditions, beliefs and lifestyles of the host

The process can be rapid, or very slow. Education, intermarriage and social exchange between immigrants and hosts will speed up the process. Cultural assimilation is slowed down if:

- immigrant groups live in segregated communities (sometimes called ghettoes)
- there are significant barriers to social mixing such as religious beliefs, differences in attitudes to women or racism and prejudice on the part or the host, immigrant group or both

The **host culture** refers to the majority, indigenous population of a country or area, e.g. white British in the UK.

Lack of cultural assimilation may have costs. It will tend to lead to a 'them and us' feeling, and lack of understanding between majority and minority groups can lead to mistrust and even fear.

In the UK, the 2016 Casey Review found that:

- 89% of people thought their community was cohesive, agreeing that their local area is a place where people from different backgrounds get on well together. This feeling of cohesiveness had risen from 80% in 2003
- 89% of people felt that they belonged 'very or fairly strongly to Britain'
- 90% of foreign nationals living in the UK already speak English 'very well'

This might suggest that in the UK at least, assimilation has been relatively successful.

In the UAE, assimilation is less likely for a number of reasons. UAE citizens make up only 11% of the total population, with immigrants making up the rest (see Figure 16):

- Emiratis tend to work in government jobs, which are separate from the global TNC jobs of Europeans and North Americans and the low-paid construction and service jobs of South Asians
- ethnically white Europeans/North Americans, Arabs and South Asians are very different and have different religions (Christian, Muslim, Hindu and Buddhist)
- there are differences in language, dress and cultural formality/informality and different views on the role of women in society
- South Asians have a very low income compared with other groups, because they do the dirty and dangerous jobs in the UAE

UAE immigrants groups, and the host Emiratis, tend to operate in very different social, economic and cultural spheres which have very little overlap.

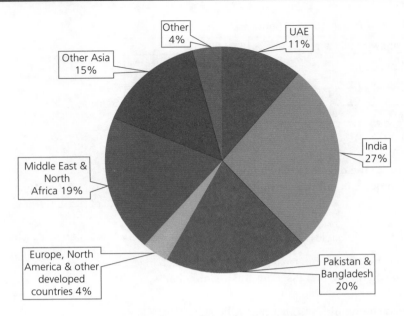

Figure 16 Nationality of the UAE population in 2015 (estimate)

Political tensions

The political tensions evident in Table 32 are caused by different perceptions of immigration in terms of its costs and benefits. This was illustrated by the question of Mexican immigration to the USA during the USA presidential election in 2016. Donald Trump stressed the costs of (often illegal) Mexican immigration and pledged to build a 'wall' along the US–Mexican border to prevent it. Others stress the economic benefits of Mexican workers, i.e. a pool of low-wage labour, helping to keep the costs of business down. In recent years, some political groups have linked immigration of Muslims to national security issues, i.e. the threat from terrorism. Table 34 summarises the perceived costs and benefits of immigration.

Knowledge check 30

Where do low-skill immigrant workers in the UAE mostly come from?

Table 34 The perceived costs and benefits of immigration for host countries

	Positive perceptions (benefits)	Negative perceptions (costs)
Social	■ Taking employment in key social services, e.g. NHS	■ Pressure on schools, the health system and other social services ■ Segregated areas of low-income migrants creates division
Cultural	■ New foods, fashions and arts ■ Greater cultural diversity makes a country more interesting and global	■ Some cultural traits are incompatible with the host culture, e.g. position of women in society
Economic	■ Fills labour shortages and skills gaps ■ Increases taxes paid to government ■ Boosts the average skill level	■ Downward pressure of wages, especially of the low paid ■ Risks displacing some host population workers
Demographic	■ Offsets an ageing population ■ Boosts fertility rates	■ Leads to overpopulation and overcrowding ■ Pressure of housing and house price rises

The costs and benefits do not only apply to the receiving country. Mexico receives about US$25 billion in **remittances** from its 12 million citizens in the USA. However, Mexico has lost many of its young people, and families are split up by emigration.

Migration opportunities

Many people would like to migrate across a national border to find better economic opportunities, a better quality of life and perhaps a safer place to live. However, migration is restricted for several reasons:

- people with low incomes will lack the financial resources to pay for travel, e.g. buses and air fares
- lower-skill, poorly educated people are less likely to migrate than higher-skill people because they have less to offer a new country
- education levels might affect the ability to apply for passports and visas

Many people face considerable obstacles, or barriers, to migration even if they want to move.

In addition, most countries have physical borders (fences, rivers, border control points) making illegal crossing impossible, and legal crossing only possible with the right documents. Most countries have immigration laws designed to prevent mass immigration and instead only allow immigration on the basis of need:

- the UK has a **points-based** system for non-EU migrants which effectively excludes low-skilled immigrants and favours investors, graduates and entrepreneurs
- Australia's system is based on filling gaps in the labour market, meaning only those with the required skills are granted work visas

How are nation states defined and how have they evolved in a globalising world?

- Nation states vary in terms of their history, geographical borders, ethnicity and the extent to which they are recognised by other nations.
- Nationalism has affected the development of nation states and colonies in the past, and continues to have an impact on migration.
- Globalisation has contributed to the rise of tax havens, which are questioned by some, and alternative state models have been adopted that attempt to reduce inequality.

Sovereignty and nation states

The concept of sovereignty is important: it means the legal right to govern a physical territory. Sovereignty has four aspects:

1. a government, organised within a territory, has authority over that territory
2. the government controls movement of people and goods across the territory's borders
3. the government and territory are recognised by other governments
4. other organisations, outside the territory, do not have higher authority

The term 'country' is unhelpful when considering sovereignty. Its meaning is vague: Wales is a 'country' but it is not sovereign, being one part of the larger UK. The word

Remittances are money sent home by immigrants to their families in their country of origin.

Exam tip

Remember that in essay questions you do need to make clear judgements in your conclusion. Having outlined a range of costs and benefits, you must then judge whether the benefits outweigh the costs. Don't be afraid to state your conclusion.

A **points-based** immigration system is one where potential immigrants are awarded points based on their skills, education level and other factors to determine whether they are needed.

is also used as in 'in the country', meaning in a rural area, and to describe specific landscapes, e.g. 'the West Country', meaning southwest England.

More useful is the term **sovereign state**. Members of the United Nations are considered sovereign states.

The term 'nation' refers to a people and their collective culture and beliefs. The term 'nation state' is used to refer to a people (nation) and the political institutions (state) that govern them.

All of this terminology is problematic in one way or another. Table 35 shows how applying terminology in a universal way is not possible.

> A **sovereign state** is a legally recognised government that exerts sovereignty over a territory.

Table 35 Problems with terminology

Some UN sovereign states are not fully sovereign	Some states are not recognised	'Nation' may not mean much
City States such as Monaco, Andorra and Lichtenstein tend to rely on other nation states for defence and aspects of border control	Taiwan and Somaliland have fully operating governments and work like states, but they are not recognised by most other sovereign states	In very culturally diverse places such as the UAE, the idea of a nation of people unified by common culture and beliefs may be quite weak

The Kurds are an example of a nation without a state (Figure 17). Kurdish people are spread across five countries in the Middle East. Kurds have a strong cultural identity as a nation, and a very long cultural history, but no state. There is a strong pro-Kurdish movement pushing for the formation of a nation state. Turkey has fought a long war against the Kurdish independence movement (the PKK) since 1984. For the Kurds to get a nation state, others would have to give up territory, which is very unlikely.

> **Exam tip**
>
> Within Topic 8, try to use the terms 'nation state' or 'sovereign state' in place of 'country'.

> **Knowledge check 31**
>
> What does the 'nation' in 'nation state' refer to?

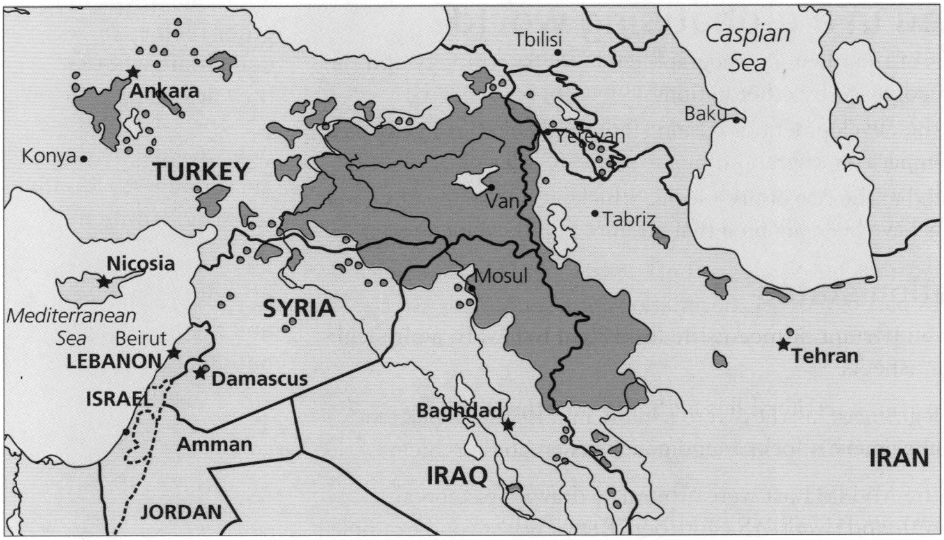

Figure 17 The Kurdish nation in the Middle East

Sovereign states are very varied culturally. Some, such as Iceland and Japan, are culturally and **linguistically** homogenous, whereas others are very diverse. Figure 18 shows the ethnicity of Iceland's and Singapore's population.

■ Most people in Iceland are ethnically Icelandic. It is a physically isolated island, with a very harsh climate not suited to most immigrants. Only in the last 10 years have some eastern Europeans migrated there for job opportunities.

■ The **indigenous** ethnic group of Singapore are Malays, but they are outnumbered by Chinese. This is because of migration from China to Singapore in the nineteenth and early twentieth centuries — particularly of traders. More recently, low-skilled migrants have arrived from India.

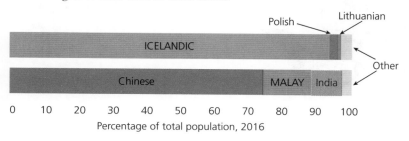

Figure 18 Ethnicity in Iceland (upper) and Singapore (lower)

National borders

The **national borders** of a sovereign state mark out the territory over which a state is sovereign. Borders are of three main types:

1 **physical**: a river, lake, mountain range or other landscape feature that provides a natural, recognisable dividing line. The coastline of island nations falls into this category

2 **evolved**: complex, sometimes intricate borders that have changed through history as territory has been fought and bargained over. Many European nation states have this type of border, and some have **enclaves**

3 **arbitrary**: drawn on a map at a set point in time, often using lines of latitude or longitude, with little or no regard for the cultural or physical geography of a place. Most date from the colonial era

Physical and evolved borders usually have some sort of **legitimacy**. This is because the border was agreed upon as part of a treaty, negotiations or a settlement after a conflict — or may simply be widely understood as the historical border between nations.

Arbitrary borders often lack legitimacy, as they were usually imposed on a place by outsiders, e.g. European colonisers. This lack of legitimacy has created problems.

Many borders in Africa and the Middle East were arbitrarily drawn by colonial administrators in the nineteenth and twentieth centuries. Kenya was a good example (Figure 19).

Linguistic refers to the languages spoken in a nation state, which can range from diverse to more universal.

Knowledge check 32

Which ethnic group forms the largest part of the population of Singapore?

A **national border** is a geographic boundary, with a legal status as the recognised limit (or start) of sovereignty over a territory.

Enclaves are parts of one sovereign state surrounded by another sovereign state.

Legitimacy is the right of a state to govern, and the acceptance of a nation of that right.

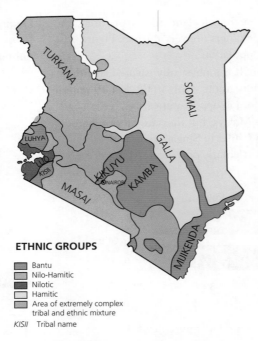

ETHNIC GROUPS

- Bantu
- Nilo-Hamitic
- Nilotic
- Hamitic
- Area of extremely complex tribal and ethnic mixture

KISII Tribal name

Figure 19 Ethnicity in Kenya, 1974

- Kenya's borders are arbitrary, drawn during the British colonial era, 1840s–1963. At the 1884–85 Berlin Conference (West Africa Conference) European colonisers formalised the borders of many African states.
- Kenya's northeastern border splits the Somali people from others in Somalia, and its southwestern border divides some nomadic Masai from others in Tanzania to the south.

Kenya descended into crisis in 2007–08 following disputed presidential elections. A political crisis quickly became an ethnic one, as some groups turned on the Kikuyu ethnic group — widely viewed as dominating politics since independence from the UK in 1963. The violence shattered an uneasy post-colonial narrative that Kenya was a unified nation and exposed long-standing ethnic tensions.

Iraq — marred by war and conflict from the 1980s onwards — is a country with three major ethno-religious groups:

- Shia Muslim Arabs in the south
- Sunni Muslim Arabs in central areas
- Kurds in the north

These groups have a long history of conflict and dispute over religion, political allegiance within Iraq and political sympathies with neighbouring countries. Governing countries such as Kenya and Iraq is a major challenge because whoever is in charge of the state is likely to be considered illegitimate by some groups.

Contested borders

In some nation states there are **separatist**, or **secessionist**, movements. The northern part of Nigeria is predominantly Muslim whereas the south is Christian or Animist.

Exam tip

Learn the names of ethnic and religious groups that dispute borders in countries such as Kenya and Iraq.

Separatist groups wish to split a nation state, and so create their own nation state — usually on ethnic and/or religious grounds.

Secession is the act of separation.

Since 2003 Boko Haram, a radical Muslim group, has fought a civil conflict with the aim of creating a Muslim state in the north. Across Africa in 2018 there were around 20 active separatist conflicts.

Around the edge of Russia, there are disputed borders. This is because:
- in 1991, following the collapse of the communist USSR (the predecessor of modern Russia) many former parts of the USSR became independent nation states
- Russian-speaking populations live in parts of Estonia, Ukraine, Georgia and Moldova
- Russia has sought to protect these Russian-speaking areas — increasingly aggressively since 2008 — which it sees as part of Russia

Russia's armed invasion of Georgia in 2008, and its violent annexation of Crimea in Ukraine in 2014, were partly to protect these Russian speakers. However, this unilateral redrawing of national borders has increased tensions with the USA and European nations because it is viewed as illegal and against international norms.

Conflict over borders can lead to large-scale migration because one group is forced out:
- Ukrainians have fled Crimea and eastern Ukraine and moved west — possibly up to 2 million of them
- about 2 million Rwandans fled the country to neighbouring Congo, Tanzania, Uganda and Burundi in 1994 following the conflict between Hutus and Tutsis in that country: a war about which ethnic groups have the right to live in, and run, Rwanda

Taiwan is an interesting case. It is only recognised by 19 UN member states, meaning it exists in a kind of limbo: Taiwan functions as a nation state, but is not recognised as one by most countries:
- in 1949 victory by the Chinese communists in the Chinese Civil War forced the defeated Nationalists to flee to the island of Taiwan (then called Formosa)
- the Nationalists, protected by the anti-communist USA, set up a government on Taiwan
- China refuses to accept the Taiwanese government as legitimate, and refuses to have diplomatic relations with any other country that does
- Taiwan has not declared independence or sovereignty because China has threatened invasion if it does

China considers Taiwan a region of China, not a 'country', and it appears as such on Chinese maps.

Nineteenth-century nationalism

Nationalism is a political viewpoint that promotes the interests of your nation state above any other interests. In the nineteenth century nationalism was linked to the growth of **empires** by European countries (Britain, France, Belgium, Germany, the Netherlands). The largest was the British Empire, which at its peak controlled over 20% of the world's territory and peoples. Table 36 explains how the expansion of empires was justified in the nineteenth century.

Knowledge check 33
In which years did Russia invade Georgia and Ukraine?

An **empire** is territory beyond a nation state's borders that has been taken by force, or purchased in some cases, over which the nation state has direct control and sovereignty.

Table 36 Nineteenth-century nationalism and empires

Mercantilism	Civilising influence
Direct control of colonies meant trade could be controlled, and other states excluded from trade, therefore maximising profit	The view that some cultures and nations were 'better' than others in terms of intelligence and level of 'civilisation', so conquering them was justified
Missionary purpose	**Environmental determinism**
The widespread view that Christianity was the only acceptable religion, and non-Christians should be converted to it	The 'scientific' theory that hot, tropical climates caused people to be less intelligent than cold, northern European climates

The views in Table 36 are not held today. Environmental determinism is a completely discredited view, with no basis at all in scientific fact. In reality, nineteenth-century empires were about conquering areas to gain access to natural resources (gold, tin, farmland) and human resources (slaves, cheap labour) and thereby making money. As European countries expanded their empires this led to conflict on two fronts:

1   In Europe the UK, France, Germany, the Netherlands, the Austro-Hungarian Empire fought each other to determine who was the most powerful 'Great Power'.

2   Conflict over territory that was being colonised in Africa, Asia, the Middle East and Caribbean between European powers and with the nations being colonised.

The British Raj

The conquest of India by the British began around 1612 and over a period of several centuries more and more of India came under British rule:

■ up to 1857, India was run by the British East India Company

■ it had a Royal Charter, and by 1803 its own army of about 250,000 men

■ it was separate from the government in London, but controlled by it

■ following the Indian Rebellion in 1857 (an unsuccessful revolt by Indians against the rule of the East India Company) the governance of India was transferred to the British Government

■ India was run, from 1858 to 1947, more like a 'country' than a colony in some ways

■ territory was directly controlled, or took the form of Princely States — these were run by an Indian Prince who was a vassal of the British Government

New nation states

The era of empire came to an end between 1945 and 1980, as European countries gave their colonies independence:

■ European countries could no longer afford to run empires, which required huge military forces to police

■ independence movements became increasingly powerful and resisting them became too costly

■ the nineteenth century justifications for empires were increasingly seen as unethical and in breach of human rights

Exam tip

If you refer to environmental determinism in the exam, make sure you make clear it is a discredited theory.

Decolonialisation accelerated in the late 1950s and 1960s, and has been called the 'Winds of Change'. Between 1956 and 1970, 38 African countries gained their independence.

Independence often came at a cost. Many newly independent African nations moved quickly towards one of two outcomes (Table 37). Both of these were costly in terms of human rights abuses, corruption and conflict. Very few African nations, even today, have become democratic nations with high levels of social and economic development. European rulers often left quickly, sometimes accompanied by violence, and the newly independent countries lacked the institutions, expertise and money needed to successfully govern a nation state for all its people.

Decolonialisation was the process of granting independence to former colonies.

Table 37 Two common outcomes of African independence

Immediate conflict (either post-independence, or as part of the fight for it)	Rule by a 'strong man' dictatorship
Guinea-Bissau 1963–74 Nigeria 1967–70 Chad 1965–79 Namibia 1966–90 Angola 1961–74	Ghana: Kwame Nkrumah 1957–66 Zimbabwe: Robert Mugabe 1980–2017 Zaire (now DRC): Mobuto Sese Seko 1966–97 Malawi: Hastings Banda 1966–94

Some post-colonial conflicts were exceptionally costly.

■ Sudan became independent from Britain in 1956. There followed the First Sudanese Civil War (1955–72) and the Second Sudanese Civil War (1983–2005) which claimed 1–2 million lives. Both conflicts had ethno-religious roots, with the Second Civil War also being about control of Sudan's southern oil fields. In 2011, the country was split into Sudan and South Sudan following a referendum. Since 2013 there has been civil war in South Sudan, displacing up to 3 million refugees and killing 50,000–300,000 as rival tribal groups (the Nuer, Murle and Kiir) fight for control of the new country.

■ The Vietnam War 1955–75 claimed the lives of 1–3 million people. Vietnam was the colony of French Indochina. It descended into conflict between the northern, communist Viet Minh and southern, nationalist State of Vietnam government in Saigon. China and the USSR backed the communists, whereas France, the USA and the UK backed Saigon: the conflict quickly became a Cold War **proxy war**, turning what might have been a relatively small civil war into a brutal geopolitical power struggle.

Wars in Sudan and Vietnam had enormous human costs, but there were other costs.

■ Economic development in both countries was halted by war, leading to widespread poverty and reliance on a few sectors that did manage to develop, i.e. oil in Sudan and post-war tourism in Vietnam.

■ Environmental costs were high. In Vietnam a defoliant called Agent Orange was used to clear vast areas of jungle of leaves, so communist forces could be spotted by US troops — this has led to a toxic legacy of pollution. In Sudan, internally displaced people led to widespread deforestation as migrants cleared trees for fuelwood and new farmland.

Knowledge check 34

Which decades saw dozens of African nations gain their independence from their European colonial rulers?

Exam tip

You will need some facts on conflicts in Sudan and Vietnam, but remember you are studying geography not history — don't get bogged down in historical detail.

A **proxy war** is one fought by two sides, who are each supported by more powerful, opposing nation states or superpowers. The more powerful nation states do not directly engage each other in the conflict.

Post-colonial migration

Since 1945 there has been migration from former colonies to the country that was once colonial master. This has been caused by a number of factors.

■ **Refugee crises**: in 1972 about 60,000 Ugandan Asians were expelled by President Idi Amin, and 27,000 came to the UK as refugees. These people were originally Indian. Their ancestors moved to Uganda as railway workers in the nineteenth century.

■ **Economic migrants**: Indonesians migrated to the Netherlands to work in the 1950s, from the former Dutch East Indies which became Indonesia in 1945. About 3% of the Dutch population today are Indonesian in origin.

■ **Family reunification**: migrants from the 1950s and 1960s were later joined by family members.

These migrations have changed the ethnic composition of former **imperial core countries**. Figure 20 shows that the UK has a large Black British (Jamaica, Nigeria, Ghana) and Asian British (India, Pakistan, Bangladesh) population and the UK has gained **cultural heterogeneity** since mass migration began in the 1950s.

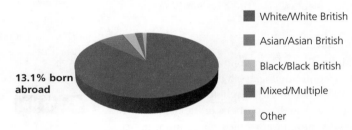

Imperial core countries means the colonial power, e.g. Britain as the colonial ruler of India, Ghana or Jamaica.

Cultural heterogeneity is the term to describe a nation state with diverse ethnicity, and therefore many people from different cultural backgrounds. Cultural diversity is a similar term.

Legend:
- White/White British
- Asian/Asian British
- Black/Black British
- Mixed/Multiple
- Other

13.1% born abroad

Figure 20 The ethnic composition of the UK in 2016

Knowledge check 35

What percentage of the UK population was born abroad in 2016?

Tax havens

There is a group of nation states that are often classified as tax havens (low-tax regime). There is no universally accepted definition of 'tax haven' but such places usually have:

■ very low personal income tax and **corporation tax** rates, or no taxes at all
■ laws making it hard to find out which companies are based in the country, i.e. secrecy
■ the legal use of **shell companies** to hide the ownership of companies or assets

Tax havens are used by both companies and wealthy **expatriates**. Walmart, the huge US retail company that owns Asda in the UK, has subsidiary companies in Curacao, Gibraltar, Barbados and Mauritius. It does not have shops in these places, which has led some people to conclude these countries help it avoid tax.

Some tax havens fall into a category that might best be described as 'not quite a nation state'. Many of these places are strongly linked to the UK, as shown in Table 38. These places are not always fully sovereign. They are small (sometimes called 'micro-states'), physically isolated/islands and depend on other countries for resources, defence or foreign policy. This lack of full sovereignty, and ambiguous status, may make it easier for them to operate opaque tax systems.

Corporation tax is tax paid by businesses, on their profits.

Shell companies are businesses that exist on paper, but have no employees or premises. They are used as devices to avoid paying taxes.

Expatriates are people from one country, e.g. the UK, who live in another country, e.g. the Bahamas, sometimes to avoid paying tax in the UK. It is often shortened to 'expats'.

Table 38 Tax havens with UK links

Ex-British colonies	Crown dependencies	British Overseas Territories
Malta, Cyprus, Bahamas, Belize	Isle of Man, Jersey, Guernsey	Bermuda, British Virgin Islands, Cayman Islands, Turks and Caicos Islands

The growth of tax havens can be linked to:

- deregulation of capital markets since the 1980s, meaning businesses, banks and investors can move money around the world — from nation state to nation state — with few controls or questions
- globalisation and the rise of truly global TNCs with parts of their businesses all over the world, with complex and hard-to-investigate internal structures
- globalisation and the rise of billionaires, who have an interest in hiding some of their wealth to protect it from taxation, and buying expensive homes in those places

Intergovernmental organisations (IGOs) such as the World Bank, International Monetary Fund and World Trade Organization have been slow to act to prevent tax abuse — which might imply they accept the situation. Non-governmental organisations (NGOs) such as the Global Alliance for Tax Justice (supported by Oxfam, ActionAid and Christian Aid, among others) have been highly critical and called for tax havens to be shut down. Table 39 considers the costs and benefits to nation states that operate as tax havens.

Table 39 Costs and benefits to nation states of tax havens

Costs	Benefits
■ Governments are deprived of tax income, so have less to spend on public services ■ Transfer mispricing is used to reduce tax paid, which affects developing and emerging countries the most ■ The reputations of TNCs may be negatively affected if they are thought to be avoiding paying tax	■ Provides income, through business and legal services, to micro-states that often have few other income streams beyond tourism ■ Allows TNCs to maximise profits, which are reinvested and therefore create more jobs and economic growth ■ Wealthy expats spend large sums of money living lavish lifestyles in tax havens, and employ local people

Inequality and alternative models

In some nation states, there has been a reaction against aspects of the **global economic system**, including:

- social and economic inequality, seen to be caused by globalisation, creating a widening gap between rich and poor
- the unfairness resulting from companies and individuals using tax havens, denying governments of vital revenue for public spending
- the lack of sustainability in terms of the environment leading to widespread deforestation, extinction of species, rising carbon emissions and climate change
- the rights of indigenous people being ignored in terms of traditional lands, culture and language

Exam tip

You need to be able to evaluate tax havens. They have costs and benefits so make sure you think about both.

Transfer mispricing works like this: Company A owns three subsidiaries, X, Y and Z. Y is in a tax haven. X sells coffee from Africa to Y at a very low price, so little tax is paid in Africa. Y sells the same coffee to Z in the USA at a very high price, so there appears to be no profit made so no tax is paid. Company Y has made a large profit, but pays no tax because it is in a tax haven. This type of scheme is usually illegal, but can be very hard to detect.

Knowledge check 36

Which developed-world nation state do many tax havens have strong historical ties to?

The **global economic system** refers to the dominant capitalist model of free markets, free trade, the profit motive and the dominance of large, global TNCs.

In both Bolivia and Costa Rica, different models for the relationship between nation and state have been tried, as shown in Table 40. In Bolivia, President Evo Morales was elected in 2006. He is indigenous Bolivian in terms of ethnicity.

Table 40 Alternative state models

Bolivia under Evo Morales	Costa Rica since 1990
■ Reduced the influence of the USA ■ Distanced Bolivia from the World Bank and IMF ■ Increased taxes on oil company profits from 18% to 82% ■ Spent additional tax-take on education and health ■ Worked successfully to increase literacy ■ Provided universal child benefit and benefits to low-income older people ■ Protected the rights of indigenous Bolivians ■ Aligned Bolivia with other left-wing governments	■ A stable multi-party democracy ■ A very high 7% of the national budget is spent on education ■ Costa Rica spends no money on defence and has no army ■ Prioritised protecting its rainforests and promoting ecotourism ■ Often said to be the 'happiest place on the planet' because of its balance of social equity and environmental protection ■ Unusually high Human Development Index for a country at its income level

Evo Morales' Bolivia is essentially a revolutionary reaction to a capitalist system perceived to have done little for ordinary Bolivians. Costa Rica's situation is different. Here, over several decades, Costa Ricans seem to have formed a collective consensus of what is important to them, and this is different from the consensus found elsewhere in the world.

What are the impacts of global organisations on managing global issues and conflict?

■ Global organisations, most significantly the United Nations, play a role in managing conflict and other global issues but not always successfully.

■ The global economy, regional and world trade are influenced by intergovernmental organisations that promote stability but have also been criticised.

■ Global environmental issues recognised by many players are both important and pressing, but finding solutions has proved challenging.

The United Nations

The United Nations (UN) was founded on 25 October 1945. Fifty-one countries agreed to adopt the United Nations Charter (Figure 21), written earlier that year when the Second World War was still ongoing. The Second World War allies (USA, UK, USSR, China and France) set up the UN. The text of Figure 21 shows that preventing another global war was foremost in the minds of those that set up the UN. However, **human rights**, gender equality, respect for international law and social progress are mentioned. The UN was therefore aiming to improve people's lives, not just stop war. Today 193 nation states are members of the UN.

Human rights refers to universal rights such as the right to free speech, the right to choose one's leaders in free elections and the right to live free from harassment. Some definitions include the right to clean drinking water, a decent income and food supply.

> **WE THE PEOPLES OF THE UNITED NATIONS DETERMINED**
>
> - to save succeeding generations from the scourge of war, which twice in our lifetime has brought untold sorrow to mankind, and
> - to reaffirm faith in fundamental human rights, in the dignity and worth of the human person, in the equal rights of men and women and nations large and small, and
> - to establish conditions under which justice and respect for the obligations arising from treaties and other sources of international law can be maintained, and
> - to promote social progress and better standards of life

Figure 21 The introduction to the 1945 UN Charter

The UN is a complex organisation with many functions and roles, as shown in Table 41. It has numerous specialist agencies with responsibility for specific issues that cover political, socio-economic and environmental spheres. Only a selection are shown in Table 41.

Table 41 The organisational structure of the UN

UN General Assembly			
All 193 member states. A debating and voting body			
Security Council			
Five permanent members (USA, UK, France, China, Russia) and ten other members (member states take turns on a rotating basis). The key decision-making body on conflict and security issues			
International Court of Justice			
Sits in The Hague, Netherlands, and puts war criminals on trial			
Specialised agencies:			
Food & Agriculture Organization (FAO): farming technology and food-supply security	International Monetary Fund (IMF): global financial stability	World Bank (WB): lending bank, which promotes economic development	World Health Organisation (WHO): disease and pandemic management, global vaccination programme

Exam tip

Learn the dates that some IGOs were founded; this is important because the aims of IGOs partly reflect the era in which they were founded.

Knowledge check 37

Which global conflict led directly to the founding of the United Nations?

The UN was set up by a very specific group of people: white, male, North Americans and Europeans who had just won the Second World War. Because of this:

- Africa, Asia and South America have always been under-represented at the UN
- women have also been under-represented (there has never been a female UN Secretary General)
- many of the UN's organisations aim to help poor people, but these people often lack a voice at the UN

In addition, even the main players at the UN have different visions about its purpose, as shown in Table 42. The USA pays 22% of the UN's annual budget and EU countries a further 35%. Arguably this gives these countries — Western capitalist democracies — a very large say in the direction and purpose of the UN.

Table 42 Competing visions of the UN

Primary purpose of the UN	Vision of:
Equality and social progress	Europeans ■ The idea of 'European liberal democracy' ■ European-style welfare state to help people
Promote trade and create wealth	USA ■ A stable world economic order, benefiting trade and TNCs ■ Capitalism is 'good' and those against it need to be converted
Prevent conflict	China and Russia ■ Neither wants the UN interfering in their countries in terms of democracy or human rights ■ Instead the UN allows powerful countries to talk to each other

Knowledge check 38

Which nation states together pay over 50% of the annual United Nations budget?

Exam tip

Be prepared to evaluate the role of the UN in the exam; it is an imperfect organisation with important, but limited, powers to intervene.

Intervention by the UN

A key purpose of the UN is the idea of **intervention** in places where problems are developing, with the aim of preventing a problem becoming a crisis. Intervention is most common when humanitarian crises are caused by famine, disease epidemics or natural disasters. UN agencies provide food, water, shelter and technical help to reduce human suffering *with the agreement* of the member states affected.

In some cases, member states *do not agree* to intervention but it is justified because of:

■ widespread and serious human rights abuses, especially **genocide**
■ conflict that risks undermining global or regional stability

In these cases there are two main types of intervention.

1 **Economic sanctions**: these affect the economy of a member state by restricting exports and/or imports, freezing the financial assets of government officials, preventing companies from international trading. The aim is to force a member state to negotiate by inflicting economic pain.

2 **Direct military intervention**: the use of **UN Peacekeeping forces** to protect civilians and keep sides in a war apart, or in some cases the use of force to try to end a conflict.

UN Peacekeeping forces, sometimes called 'blue berets' after the light blue colour of their military berets, are armed forces and/or police from UN member states but operating under the UN flag. The UN does not have its own armed forces, it relies on member states contributing troops, police and military hardware.

Economic sanctions have a mixed track record. The system of **apartheid** in South Africa was condemned by the UN in 1973 as a 'crime against humanity' and further condemnations were made in 1978 and 1983. Some companies, and many sporting events, boycotted South Africa but change was slow to come. In 1987 the UN agreed to voluntary sanctions banning oil exports to South Africa. With hindsight, stronger economic sanctions may have ended apartheid sooner.

Intervention means action by the UN within the territory of a member state, to prevent conflict, economic crisis, famine, disease epidemics, human rights abuses and other issues. The UN Assembly and Security Council pass resolutions which provide the legal basis for intervention.

Genocide is a deliberate attempt to exterminate an ethnic or religious group: the Nazi extermination of Jews is an example.

Apartheid was a set of laws in South Africa that separated white and black South Africans and gave different rights to each. It was widely considered racist and an abuse of human rights. It ended in 1993.

In 2006 the UN passed United Nations Security Council Resolution 1696 putting economic sanctions on Iran. These were strengthened in 2007 and 2010.

- The aim was to force Iran to stop its nuclear power and nuclear weapons programme.
- The world feared a nuclear-armed Iran would lead to war in the Middle East.
- Foreign assets were frozen, oil exports were banned and imports of even basic medical equipment were stopped.

The crippling impact of this forced Iran to negotiate and the sanctions were ended in 2016, with Iran agreeing to end its nuclear programme. As of 2018, President Trump had re-imposed the sanctions, but the situation remains unpredictable.

Since 1945 the UN has used peacekeepers 56 times. The UN has peacekeepers in the Middle East and on the India–Pakistan border, which have been there since 1948 and 1949, respectively. There were 16 peacekeeping missions ongoing as of 2018.

UN peacekeepers have been involved in the Democratic Republic of Congo (DRC) since 1999, intervening in the Second Congo War. The war is a fight between DRC government forces under President Laurent Kabila and various rebel groups under the RCD (Rally for Congolese Democracy) flag. At stake is control of the DRC and its vast mineral wealth — including **conflict minerals** such as gold, diamonds and coltan (used in mobile phones). The war has an ethnic dimension, and has spilled over into Uganda, Rwanda and Burundi.

- In 2017 there were 18,300 UN peacekeepers in the DRC operating as MONUSCO (United Nations Organization Stabilization Mission in the Democratic Republic of the Congo).
- More than 30 member states have contributed troops.
- The total cost has been over US$9 billion since 1999.

Table 43 considers the successes and failures of the UN action.

Table 43 Evaluating UN Peacekeeping in the DRC

Successes	Failures
■ The situation may have been worse without UN involvement ■ The UN may have prevented wider, direct involvement by other countries, i.e. an African World War ■ The UN has collected evidence that may lead to war crimes trials ■ Humanitarian help and aid has been provided by the UN, protected by peacekeepers	■ Despite 20 years of UN action, the war still raged in Ituri and Kivu regions in 2018 ■ DRC is more dependent than ever on war-lord controlled conflict minerals ■ Over 5 million dead, plus 200 UN peacekeepers ■ Income in DRC is about US$400 per person per year ■ Shocking war crimes, involving child soldiers and sexual violence, have been widespread

Intervention by nation states

Not all interventions are made by the UN. Sometimes individual nation states, or coalitions, act outside direct UN control. An example is the UK's intervention in Sierra Leone (a former UK colony) in 2000, considered to be a **failed state** at that time.

Conflict minerals are high-value minerals and ores, such as gold and diamonds, that have caused war as opposing groups fight to control mining and trade.

A **failed state** is a nation state where governance has broken down and there is no effective state that can protect the nation's people. Basic services (water, health) have collapsed and the lack of security risks people's lives on a daily basis.

- Sierra Leone descended into Civil War in 1991, and by 1999 more than 50,000 were dead.
- The UN became involved in 1999, but this intervention failed and the UK decided to step in.
- Operation Palliser, with 1,200 troops, naval and air support, drove rebel forces back from Freetown, the capital city, and led to a ceasefire.
- UK intervention saved the UN mission in Sierra Leone.

By 2002, the war was over and the country has made progress since. Several war criminals were prosecuted, including Charles Taylor (rebel leader), who was convicted of war crimes in 2012. The UK's intervention is viewed as having been highly successful. Table 44 summarises some other recent interventions.

Table 44 Examples of interventions

The USA's 'War on Terror' since 2001	UK and France in Libya, 2011	Russia's intervention in Ukraine, 2014
Military actions around the world against Islamist terrorists (Al Qaeda, Taliban, Islamic State) in response to the 9/11 attacks on the World Trade Center in New York	An airforce bombing campaign in support of rebel forces fighting the government forces of Colonel Gadaffi. In the context of the 2011 **Arab Spring**	Russian invasion of Crimea and western Ukraine, justified as protecting ethnic Russians but viewed in the West as a breach of international law and the sovereignty of Ukraine
Impact on geopolitical relations and political stability		
<ul><li>Viewed as 'demonising' the Muslim religion</li><li>Turned some Muslims in Western countries into radical Islamists</li><li>Contributed to the rise of Islamic State — as an extremist response to the 'War on Terror'</li><li>Made Middle Eastern countries 'take sides', i.e. for or against the USA</li></ul>	<ul><li>Disagreement among NATO members over how to act</li><li>Disintegration of governance in Libya</li><li>Refugee and humanitarian crisis in Libya as no effective government has emerged since 2011</li></ul>	<ul><li>Economic and political crisis in Ukraine</li><li>Deterioration in relations between Russia and the EU/USA</li><li>Economic sanctions imposed on Russia</li><li>Build up of **NATO** forces on its borders with Russia</li></ul>

Global economic management

Three global IGOs were set up in the 1940s, whose aims were economic. These are:

- **World Bank (WB) in 1945**: lending money for economic development projects, to developing and emerging countries
- **IMF in 1945**: promotion of global economic stability, and helping countries in economic difficulty to recover
- **World Trade Organization (WTO) in 1948**: promotion of free trade, based on the idea that more trade means more economic growth, and wealth. It was known as the General Agreement on Tariffs and Trade (GATT) before 1996

All three still exist today, and continue to be key pillars of the global economic system. However, these IGOs:

- promote a Western capitalist model: they are in favour of TNCs, profits, trade and the accumulation of wealth

■ were not supported by communist countries during the Cold War, e.g. Cuba, China and the USSR

Since the end of the Cold War in 1991, the IMF, WB and WTO have become more dominant in the global economic system. A key question is whose interests have been best served by these IGOs? Figure 22 shows per capita income by region between 1870 and 2016.

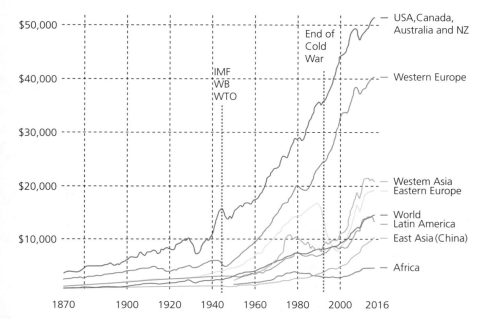

Figure 22 Per capita income 1870–2016, by global region

Figure 22 suggests:

■ the countries that set up (and still run) the UN, IMF, WB and WTO in the 1940s have seen the largest rises in income since the 1940s
■ the gap between the rich 'West' and 'the rest' has increased since the 1940s
■ communist eastern Europe saw good income growth between 1945 and 1990, but this collapsed as the Cold War ended in 1991 and has only just recovered
■ China (eastern Asia) has grown strongly since 2000
■ Latin America, and especially Africa, have made much slower, limited progress

It could be argued that the very countries that set up the global economic and political system in 1945 — which still persists today — have been the ones to benefit most from free trade and borrowing money to invest in industry and infrastructure.

Borrowing and debt

A key UN aim is the promotion of economic and social development in developing countries. The World Bank gave loans for development purposes to developing countries, as did individual nation states and commercial banks. Borrowed money was invested in infrastructure (roads, ports and electricity generation), industry and social services such as hospitals and schools.

Knowledge check 41

Which global region, shown on Figure 22, has made the least economic progress since 1945?

By the 1980s it was clear that this 'lending for development' had, in many cases, not worked. Developing countries had large, unpayable debts and huge annual debt interest payments. This was often called 'Third World Debt'.

Help came in the form of **Structural Adjustment Policies** (SAPs) via the 1996 Heavily Indebted Poor Country Initiative (HIPC) and, after 2006, the Multilateral Debt Relief Initiative.

These debt relief schemes, run by the IMF, involved developing countries giving up some **economic sovereignty** by agreeing to a programme of:

- reduced spending on health, education and other social programmes
- opening up their economies to foreign investment by TNCs
- adopting free-trade policies
- privatising government-run industries

The HIPC scheme lasted for 6 years, after which some or all of the country's debt was cancelled. Table 45 evaluates the HIPC scheme undertaken by Uganda. Critics of the HIPC state that some unsustainably high-debt countries, such as Kenya, have not qualified for the HIPC. Further, the economic reform programme forces a Western capitalist model on countries, which may increase inequality.

Table 45 Pros and cons of HIPC in Uganda

Pros	Cons
■ Starting in 2000, debt eventually fell from around US$5 billion to US$1.1 billion by 2007 ■ Money saved by reduced debt payments was put into a Poverty Action Fund, providing access to clean water for 2.2 million people ■ Poverty levels fell from 55% to 25% from 1993 to 2012 ■ Education enrolment increased from 62% to 87%	■ No debt was cancelled until the full 6-year, painful reform programme was finished ■ Poverty may have increased during the 6-year programme, but fell after it ■ Remaining debts, even after 6 years, may be unsustainably high: 17% of GDP in Uganda's case in 2013

Trade blocs

Almost all nation states are members of global IGOs including the World Bank, IMF, WTO and the United Nations. These organisations provide frameworks for international trade, finance, lending and borrowing, as well as issues such as migration.

However, in many cases, groups of countries within particular regions have decided to cooperate more closely by setting up their own regional IGOs, especially covering trade:

- **NAFTA**: the North American Free Trade Agreement, set up in 1992, is a free-trade area in goods between Mexico, Canada and the USA
- **ASEAN**: the Association of South East Asian Nations formed in 1967 to promote the interests of member states and adopt free-trade policies between members (Myanmar, Laos, Cambodia, Vietnam, Thailand, Indonesia, Philippines, Brunei and Singapore)
- **EU**: the European Union has 28 member states (27 when the UK leaves) and was founded as a trading bloc, but has evolved into a political and social union with free movement of goods, services and people between member states

Structural Adjustment Policies (SAPs) are economic policies such as government spending cuts and trade liberalisation, imposed by the IMF on indebted countries. The IMF effectively controls economic policy in the country until debt is reduced to manageable levels.

Economic sovereignty exists when a nation state makes its own economic decisions, without outside interference or influence by organisations such as the IMF.

Exam tip

There is no right answer to a question such as 'has the HIPC scheme been successful?', because it has both pros and cons.

Most regional IGOs are based on trade, or in some cases military co-operation, e.g. NATO. The EU is unusual because of the political aspect of cooperation and freedom of movement.

The atmosphere and biosphere

IGOs involved in **global governance** focused on economic, social and conflict resolution in the 1940s and 1950s. Beginning in the late 1960s a new focus emerged: that of global environmental issues. This came about for several reasons:

- rapidly rising world population, passing 3 billion around 1960, and growing fears of food and water shortages
- issues such as air pollution, water pollution and toxic chemicals in the food chain became too serious to ignore
- the conquest of outer space provided images of Earth from above, showing people just how small and isolated our planet is

CITES, the Convention on International Trade in Endangered Species, was set up in 1973 by the International Union for the Conservation of Nature (IUCN) — itself founded in 1948 on the advice of **UNESCO**. IUCN is not part of the UN, but works very closely with it. CITES is an international treaty that bans international trade in 37,000 **endangered** plants and animals in an attempt to protect the **biosphere**. As of 2018, 183 nation states are members. Table 46 evaluates CITES. It is widely seen as having been successful in protecting some species, but has its problems.

Table 46 Evaluating CITES

Pros	Cons
Membership is almost universal, and there is international cooperation, which reduces illegal trade	Species, not ecosystems, are protected so issues such as deforestation are not addressed. Global Warming could undermine it
Protected species include a wide variety of plants and animals from across the world	Relies on countries, many of which are poor, putting in place their own monitoring and policing systems
Some key successes, e.g. reducing the ivory trade and halting the decline of African Elephants up to 2005, although illegal poaching has increased in the last decade	Species have to be under threat to be 'on the list' by which time the problem may be too serious to solve
CITES has raised awareness of high-profile threatened species, e.g. the snow leopard	Economic interests get in the way, e.g. failure to protect bluefin tuna and many shark species because of pressure from commercial fishing

The 1987 Montreal Protocol is arguably the most remarkable example of an international environmental agreement. It was designed to deal with the issue of **ozone** depletion in the stratosphere.

- In the 1930s chemists invented new colourless, odourless gases called CFCs (chlorofluorocarbons) which proved very useful in refrigeration and as propellants.
- These were widely used in industry and in household products from the 1950s onwards.

Global governance refers to efforts, at an international level, to manage issues such as conflict, human rights abuses, environmental issues, poverty and inequality.

UNESCO is the United Nations Educational, Scientific and Cultural Organization.

Endangered means a species that is threatened with extinction because of human threats, such as over-hunting or deforestation.

The **biosphere** is the living layer of the Earth; the ecosystems that live beneath the atmosphere and above the lithosphere.

Ozone is a form of oxygen (O_3) in the stratosphere. It helps filter out harmful incoming ultraviolet light from the sun, which causes cancer in animal species.

- In 1973 scientists first theorised that CFCs could destroy stratospheric ozone.
- In 1985 the British Antarctic Survey discovered a 'hole' — really a thinning — of the ozone layer above Antarctica.

Only two years later the leaders of developed countries agreed to ban CFCs, and help emerging and developing countries move towards replacing their use. Virtually no country argued against the ban, and evidence of 'cheating the agreement' has been minimal. On current trends the ozone layer will be fully recovered by 2070 (Figure 23).

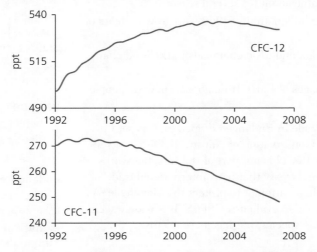

Figure 23 Levels of two CFCs in the atmosphere 1992–2008 (ppt = parts per trillion)

The wider issue of global warming, managed internationally by the UNFCCC (United Nations Framework Convention on Climate Change), has proved much harder to gain universal agreement on compared with the ozone issue:

- it was first discussed by world leaders at the UN Earth Summit in Rio de Janeiro in 1992, but no direct action was taken
- in 1997 the Kyoto Protocol treaty agreed carbon emissions cuts for developed nations, but these were small and some countries — the USA, Russia, Canada and Australia — did not agree
- the 2015 Paris Agreement (often called 'COP21') made more significant progress, among all nations, with agreed carbon emissions cuts. Most scientists see this progress as a good start, but not a solution that will halt or reverse global warming

The oceans and water

Other aspects of the global environment are managed internationally.

- Open oceans are managed by UNCLOS (United Nations Convention on the Law of the Sea) which includes the MARPOL convention on marine pollution from ships. This bans dumping of garbage from ships, and 'bilging' which means cleaning ship's tanks with sea water while at sea.
- On land, water resources such as lakes, rivers and aquifers which are **transboundary** are governed by the Helsinki and Berlin Rules. These are legal frameworks for sharing water resources fairly between nation states.

Exam tip

As part of your revision, think carefully about why some environmental treaties and agreements have been successful, whereas others have been less so.

Knowledge check 42

How many years passed between the discovery that CFCs could damage ozone and the signing of the Montreal Protocol?

Transboundary water resources are those which are shared across one or more international borders.

- In 2005 a major scientific report on the state of global ecosystems, called the MEA (Millennium Ecosystem Assessment), was published. It is an example of global scientific cooperation to monitor the state of the world's environment and the impact of pollution, deforestation and other threats.

There are many examples of global cooperation on the environment. These are often successful, but in many cases are a compromise rather than an ideal solution to global environmental issues.

Managing Antarctica

Antarctica is a **global common** and the only land-mass on Earth not owned by a nation state. It has never been inhabited, so there is no Antarctic 'nation'. Parts of the continent have been claimed by nation states (Figure 24). Today Antarctica is governed by the Antarctic Treaty System (ATS) which came into force in 1961 and has been signed by 53 nation states. The ATS:

- put 'on hold' the territorial claims shown in Figure 24
- set aside Antarctica for peaceful, scientific purposes — military forces are banned
- banned all resource extraction (fossil fuels, ores and minerals) and strictly manages fishing and tourism
- the results of science carried out in Antarctica are shared, and all areas are accessible to all scientists

Antarctica has problems, including over-fishing, pressure from cruise-ship tourism, global warming and localised pollution from scientific bases. However, overall it is a model of peaceful scientific cooperation.

> **Global commons** are areas of the Earth which are not owned by nation states: they include the open oceans, Antarctica and the atmosphere.

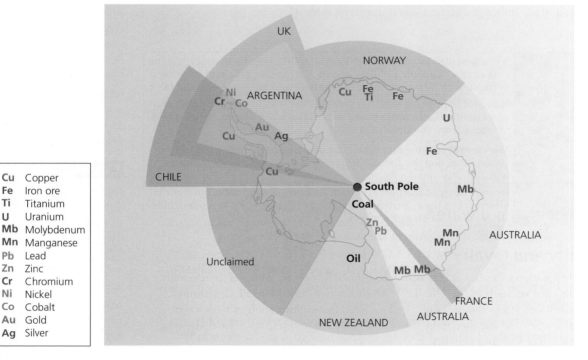

Cu	Copper
Fe	Iron ore
Ti	Titanium
U	Uranium
Mb	Molybdenum
Mn	Manganese
Pb	Lead
Zn	Zinc
Cr	Chromium
Ni	Nickel
Co	Cobalt
Au	Gold
Ag	Silver

Figure 24 Territorial claims and mineral reserves in Antarctica

Antarctica is essentially a 'world park'. There is an argument for similar international action on other 'world parks' such as:

- the Arctic Ocean, threatened by global warming and future oil and gas exploitation
- remaining tropical rainforests (Amazonia, the Congo Basin, southeast Asia) which act as the 'lungs of the planet'
- oceans, threatened by plastic pollution and over-fishing

This kind of action is unlikely because some of these places are sovereign territory, and nation states would have to give up sovereignty to allow international management.

What are the threats to national sovereignty in a more globalised world?

- Despite globalisation, national identity and the force of nationalism remains powerful in some places and has seen a resurgence in others.
- Globalisation challenges traditional perceptions of national identity due to foreign ownership of assets and complex business structures.
- Some nation states experience disunity and political tensions, even leading to calls for independence for some nations.

National identity and nationalism

Despite decades of globalisation, nationalism remains a powerful force. People's national identity is often very strong and can be a source of pride. Many people readily identify with **national symbols**, although increasingly they also identify with global brands such as the logos of Apple, Facebook, Nike and Samsung. National identity is reinforced in a number of different ways, shown in Table 47.

Table 47 National identity in the UK

Education	'Fundamental British Values' taught in UK schools: democracy, the rule of law, individual liberty and mutual respect for and tolerance of those with different faiths and beliefs and for those without faith
Sport	National teams use national symbols such as the rose (rugby) and lions (football, cricket) as well as strips and kits using colours and symbols from the Union Flag
Political parties	The Conservative Party logo is an oak tree in the colours of the Union Flag, and the Labour Party uses a red rose — all symbols with national links
Brands	Brands such as Burberry, British Airways, Paul Smith and Rimmel often stress their 'Britishness', or stress their links to a particular UK location, such as London

Identity and loyalty

Defining a nation's identity is very difficult, especially for one which is increasingly culturally diverse, such as the UK. Table 48 shows two definitions of 'Britishness'. Both definitions stress the importance of national institutions such as Parliament, the legal system and the monarchy (the Crown). These institutions uphold ideals of democracy, freedom and equality so are seen as important to national identity.

National symbols are usually visual images linked strongly to sovereign states and nations, such as flags, coats of arms, national colours, national football strips, flowers and animals. Most are bold and instantly recognisable.

Exam tip

National identity is a difficult term to define, so make sure you learn a definition to use in the exam.

Outside the UK, people are loyal to other systems of governance such as the 5th Republic in France which has a president rather than a monarch as Head of State. In the USA people tend to be loyal to the national government in Washington DC and their home state in equal measure, because of the federal nature of the US republic.

Knowledge check 43

How is 'Britishness' taught in UK schools?

Table 48 Definitions of 'Britishness'

UK Government, Home Office (2002)	'To be British seems to us to mean that we respect the laws, the elected parliamentary and democratic political structures, traditional values of mutual tolerance, respect for equal rights and mutual concern ... to be British is to respect those over-arching specific institutions, values, beliefs and traditions that bind us all'
Commission for Racial Equality (2005)	'Britishness' is organised around the following dimensions: geography, people, national symbols, citizenship, values and attitudes, cultural habits and behaviour, language and historical achievements.

There are more subjective identities referred to as '**national character**'. Aspects of national character are hard to define, but their absence (or the presence of other, unusual characteristics) can indicate people are 'foreign'. Frequently the most obvious national characteristics are used in the form a national stereotype. Figure 25 is part national stereotype, part national character. It is based on a survey carried out by Tetley Tea in 2016. National character is important in understanding why people feel a collective identity.

National character describes the personality of people in a nation, including manners, humour, formality/informality in different social and business situations, expression of emotions and many other cultural characteristics.

- People may feel they have shared experience of 'behaving the same way' by recognising characteristics of themselves in other people.
- People can feel strongly about defending aspects of their national identity that feel important — such as democracy, a free and fair legal system, or even a physical landscape they value, such as the English countryside.

1. Wearing summer clothing at the first sight of sun
2. Apologising automatically
3. Ability to talk at length about the weather
4. Making a cup of tea in response to a crisis
5. Finding queue-jumping the ultimate crime
6. Forming a queue for pretty much anything
7. The typically British 'stiff upper lip'
8. Grumbling throughout a meal, but not telling staff so as not to cause a fuss
9. Making sarcastic/dry jokes
10. Finding the American forwardness 'a bit much'
11. Avoiding eye contact on public transport
12. Insisting the other person goes through the door first

Figure 25 Twelve 'British Characteristics' from a 2016 survey of Britons

National identity is complex. According to the long-running British Social Attitudes Survey:

- in 1992, 62% of people living in England described themselves as 'British' and about 30% 'English'
- by 2012 'British' had declined to 44% and 'English' increased to 44%

This shift might suggest the broader national identity of belonging to the United Kingdom is declining in favour of a more local 'Englishness' — perhaps as a result of Scotland and Wales gaining their own parliaments in 1999.

Similar surveys in the EU, by Eurobarometer, have found:
- only about 2% of citizens identify themselves as European only
- about 5% identify as European first followed by their actual nationality
- 45% identify as their nationality first, and as European second
- 40% identify as only their nationality

These results suggest that despite decades of European Union political, economic and social integration, the idea of nationality is very strong and resists erosion.

Other results are harder to interpret. Figure 26 shows results from a 2016 Pew Global Attitudes Survey which asked people how important being born in their country is to being part of that nation. Results range from 8% in Sweden to 52% in Hungary. Possible explanations include:
- high levels of recent immigration, reducing the feeling that 'being born here' is important
- the degree of globalisation and engagement with the world economy
- the degree of ethnic and cultural diversity (or homogeneity) in the country

Having been born in our country is very important for being truly [survey country nationality]

USA	32%
Canada	21%
Hungary	52%
Greece	50%
Italy	42%
Poland	42%
Spain	34%
UK	32%
France	25%
Netherlands	16%
Germany	13%
Sweden	8%
Japan	50%
Australia	13%

Spring 2016 Global Attitudes Survey, Pew

Figure 26 Results from a 2016 Pew Global Attitudes Survey

'Made in Britain'?

To some extent, products and brands are linked to national identity. Many countries are known worldwide for the goods and services they produce (Table 49) and this can be a source of national pride as well as a source of income and employment.

Exam tip

National identity is very subjective, so having some numerical data from surveys of attitudes will help you provide evidence in the exam.

Knowledge check 44

What percentage of European citizens identify themselves as 'European only'?

Some countries have particular strengths in certain economic sectors, as Table 49 shows.

Table 49 High value global brands for three countries (brand value rank from Interbrand 2017 top 100 global brands)

USA Technology	Germany Automotive	France Fashion
Apple (1st)	Mercedes-Benz (9th)	Louis Vuitton (19th)
Google (2nd)	BMW (13th)	Hermes (32nd)
Microsoft (3rd)	Audi (38th)	L'Oreal (39th)
Amazon (5th)	VW (40th)	Cartier (65th)
Facebook (8th)	Porsche (48th)	Dior (95th)

The UK has high-value, well-known global brands that are considered 'British' but which, in many cases, are now owned by foreign campanies

- Rolls-Royce Motor Cars has been owned by German TNC BMW since 1998
- Jaguar Land Rover has been owned by the Indian TNC Tata since 2008, which has also owned Tetley Tea since 2000
- Cadbury chocolate was bought by US company Kraft Foods (now called Mondolez International) in 2010
- Chinese companies own (wholly or in part) Pizza Express, Hamley's and Weetabix

Globalisation has created complex patterns of ownership and production, meaning that the idea of 'Made in Britain' is no longer as simple as a British company making products in a British factory. This may not matter in terms of national identity, but perhaps the erosion of a sense of owning and making globally valued products may matter to some people.

Non-national ownership

Increasingly land in nation states is owned by foreigners. A very good example is London. There are good reasons why foreign companies, and individuals, might want to buy London property:

- as a world city and global hub, the value of land and buildings is likely to rise in the future, making property a good investment
- it may be hard for tax authorities in the home country to get their hands on assets owned in London (this is one reason why around 1,000 central London properties are owned by wealthy Russians)
- there is prestige in owning prime real estate on London's smartest streets

There are also negatives to this foreign ownership:

- it is possible that some of the money invested was earned illegally in foreign countries, and buying London property is a way of hiding this money
- many foreign-owned properties are not occupied, but demand for them pushes up prices for everyone, thereby reducing property supply for local Londoners
- between 35,000 and 40,000 properties in London are owned by **offshore companies**, making the actual buyer hard to trace

The small Middle-Eastern country of Qatar is one of the biggest property owners. The Qatar Investment Authority (QIA) is a government-owned company that in 2015 bought the owner of Canary Wharf, Songbird Estates, for £2.6 billion. QIA also owns

> **Knowledge check 45**
>
> Which country is the parent company of UK car maker Jaguar Land Rover from?

> **Offshore companies** are those based abroad, often in tax havens and often with complex ownership structures.

The Shard, Harrods, the Olympic Village and Claridge's Hotel, as well as One Hyde Park, Camden Market, and an estimated £1 billion of property in Mayfair. It makes the government of Qatar the biggest property owner in London (Figure 27).

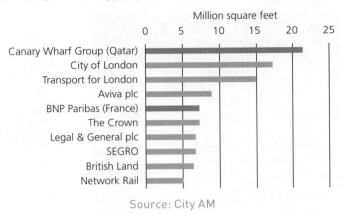

Source: City AM

Figure 27 The ten largest property owners in London, 2017

Westernisation

There is general acceptance that 'Western' cultural values are the dominant ones globally. As the USA is arguably a hyperpower, the dominant Western values are American ones: hence the term '**Americanisation**', namely:

- more informality in personal and business relations
- directness of speech
- use of American words and spellings
- spread of American film, TV and media
- spread of fast food
- a culture of consumption, and the idea that wealth is important and should be a key life aim

American culture is spread particularly by TNCs involved in media (Disney, CNN, Fox, Warner Brothers, Netflix) and retailing/fast food (Walmart, Nike, McDonalds, KFC, Coca-Cola). These TNCs and their brands are ubiquitous. Many of them are linked, through slogans, advertising and sponsorship, to American values. Figure 28 presents an interesting expression of American values, shown as three rights, each of which comes at a 'price'. This suggests that the benefits of American capitalism have to be earned.

> The first is Individual Freedom and the price for that is Self-Reliance.

> The second is Equality of Opportunity, and the price for that is Competition.

> The third is The American Dream, the opportunity for a better life and a higher standard of living. The price for the American Dream has traditionally been Hard Work.

Figure 28 American values expressed on the US website vintageamericanways.com

Americanisation refers to a shift in cultural values and attitudes towards ones that have American characteristics.

Exam tip

Americanisation and Westernisation are linked, but are not the same thing. Americanisation is a more specific form of Westernisation: make sure you recognise the difference.

'Westernisation' doesn't have to mean 'Americanisation'. Europe is capitalist but especially in the northern European **Nordic countries** people have to pay a lot of their income in tax, usually 40–50% versus about 25% in the USA. The tax is used to:

- provide housing, healthcare and education
- provide benefits for low-income and vulnerable people

These countries believe in social or collective good as much as they do in individual rights and responsibility. This is sometimes called 'European social democracy' and is very different to the USA's 'individual responsibility' model. Some Europeans are very opposed to the American model, believing it creates a very unequal society and would undermine their national identity of looking after everyone.

Nationalist movements

Nationalism can involve a whole sovereign state, but often it involves people who consider themselves to be a separate nation within a sovereign state which they no longer want to be part of. This is **separatism** or secessionism. There are many reasons behind the desire to separate:

- nations of people — Scots, Catalans, Basques, Québécois — consider themselves culturally different from the majority of the nation state
- minority nations feel their needs are ignored or unrepresented by the majority
- separatists may feel their political views or values are different, and deserve to be recognised as such
- in order to preserve a culture and traditions a nation may feel it needs its own nation state

In some cases, nations were deliberately oppressed by the majority but this often backfired and intensified demands for independence.

- **Russification in the USSR**: a policy of only teaching Russian in schools across the USSR, not traditional languages, and discouraging religions such as Islam.
- **Francoist Spain**: under the dictator General Franco in Spain, 1936–75, regional languages (Basque, Catalan, Galician) were banned in schools and some cultural traditions such as bullfighting and flamenco dancing were promoted as 'national' even though they were not traditional across the whole of Spain.

Both Scotland (2014) and Catalonia (2017) have held referendums on splitting from the UK and Spain, respectively (neither resulted in independence). In both cases, those arguing for independence also argued for staying in the EU trading bloc after independence. This is an interesting standpoint:

- independence would mean gaining national sovereignty, only to immediately give it up because the EU is a 'higher power' exercising sovereignty in many areas
- Catalonia and Scotland would be small, so it makes sense to be part of a larger economic bloc
- existing EU members would probably block membership, because it could encourage other nationalist movements and further fragment the EU

Separatist nationalism can be violent. The **Basque** nationalist group ETA (Euskadi Ta Askatasuna/Basque Homeland and Liberty) was founded in 1958. It gradually became more political and by 1968 was an armed group. Between 1968 and 2010 ETA killed more than 800 people and injured thousands, including police, soldiers

The **Nordic countries** are Norway, Sweden, Denmark, Finland (collectively Scandinavia) and Iceland.

Knowledge check 46

American TNCs from which economic sectors are very influential in spreading 'Americanisation'?

Separatism means splitting a nation of people, usually a minority, from a larger sovereign state to create a new nation state.

There are around 2–3 million **Basque** people in France and Spain, and perhaps 700,000 speak Basque. The Basque language is 'isolated' in that it has almost nothing in common with other European languages — even word order and sentence construction are different from both French and Spanish.

and civilians across Spain. In 2017 it gave up all of its weapons and became a purely political organisation. ETA was often called a terrorist organisation, although to many Basques it was an organisation of freedom fighters.

Globalisation tensions

While there are nationalist movements in some countries threatening to split sovereign states apart, there are also political tensions in **emerging nations** that could have similar results.

This political disunity has many causes but it is often linked to globalisation's costs and benefits:

- the income difference between factory workers and business owners is large, and inequality very obvious
- emerging countries, while getting wealthier, often lack a welfare state to help poor and marginalised people
- the environmental costs of rapid urbanisation and industrialisation have created polluted air, water and land so overall quality of life is often low

Overall in emerging countries the costs and benefits of globalisation have an uneven pattern, with some people reaping large benefits and many others experiencing costs. Table 50 shows some of the outcomes of political tensions in emerging countries.

Table 50 Tensions in emerging countries

Brazil: corruption	Chile: inequality	China: pollution
■ In 2015–16 there were widespread protests against corrupt politicians in Brazil ■ Up to 7 million people took part ■ President Lula da Silva (2003–11) was charged with corruption and bribery in 2015 ■ His successor, Dilma Rousseff, was charged with corruption in 2016, accused of stealing money from the government-run oil company Petrobras	■ In 2017 2 million people protested against changes to pensions ■ The privatisation of the pension system is seen as having benefited the rich, and penalised the poor ■ Women have been especially badly hit, and there are calls for the whole system to be government-run and made fairer	■ In July 2010, about 10,000 residents of Qidong protested against a planned waste pipeline that would dump industrial waste water into the sea, from the Japanese Oji Paper Company factory ■ In 2015, 1,000 people protested on the streets of Shanghai against the construction of a new chemical plant ■ A similar number protested in the same year in Tianjin, claiming a steel factory's emissions were causing cancer

Protests in China are rare:

- they are usually brutally ended by police and protesters are arrested
- reference to protests on the internet and social media are removed by censors
- they are not reported in the Chinese media
- the current Premier, Xi Jinping, has cracked down on them especially harshly

The very fact that people are prepared to risk openly protesting in China suggests they feel they have little to lose, because their concerns are so deeply felt.

Knowledge check 47

Which sovereign states do the Basque nation mostly live in?

Emerging nations are rapidly growing, middle-income ones — such as the BRICs (Brazil, Russia, India and China) — that often have a widening gap between the rich and poor.

Exam tip

Learn some of the detail in Table 50, so you have a range of examples of protests showing political divisions.

Weak national identity

There are a number of countries where national identity is very weak and sovereignty is non-existent or collapsing. These countries are often called failed states because:

- territory is contested, and controlled by more than one group of people using force
- there is no universally recognised sovereign body, i.e. government
- public services are not provided
- the country does not interact with other countries in a normal way, i.e. trade and diplomacy

Knowledge check 48

What type of issue often leads to protests against the government or companies in China?

In 2018 failed states included Somalia, the Central African Republic, Syria, Yemen, South Sudan and the Democratic Republic of Congo. Myanmar and Afghanistan also had many failed-state features. In these countries, the population can often be divided into three groups, as shown in Table 51.

Table 51 Contrasting groups in failed states

Politically and economically powerful elite	Foreign investor groups	Wider population
■ Politicians, government officials and business owners ■ Have large personal wealth, security guards and political protection ■ Wealth acquired through corruption and illegal activities	■ TNCs exploiting oil, minerals and precious metals ■ Mining rights sold by corrupt government officials ■ Often protected by the elite, who gain income from the TNCs ■ Most profits leave the country	■ 50–80% of people live in extreme poverty ■ Many are subsistence farmers, or informal labourers ■ Public services are almost non-existent and many people rely on NGOs for basic needs

Summary

- Globalisation has contributed to an increase in both international and internal migration, but migrant population has significant variations between countries, and policies towards immigration differ.
- The majority of migration is linked to economic factors and the desire for better incomes, but the ability to migrate for work is variable. Conflict also drives migration.
- The impacts of immigration can be both positive and negative, with economic and demographic benefits often offset by political and cultural costs, leading to changes in policy towards immigration and immigrants.
- Sovereignty is a key political idea, but the historical geography of sovereign states means sovereignty is often disputed and the borders of a sovereign state may not be recognised by all.
- The colonial era, and the nationalism that accompanied it, is important in terms of understanding conflict in some nations and patterns of international migration.
- Some sovereign states operate as tax havens, and their existence is controversial: in some cases governments have attempted to create states which are different from the dominant free-market capitalist model.
- The United Nations, and other IGOs, play a key role in global conflict management and managing environmental issues, but their success is disputed: sovereign states can also act independently of global IGOs.
- IGOs also manage trade and economic stability, both globally and regionally, but intervention in indebted developing countries has had variable results.
- Nationalism is linked to the complex idea of national identity, but this idea is challenged by globalisation and complex patterns of property and business ownership.
- Many nation states are unified but many are not and this creates political forces that can lead to independence movements, as well as the existence of failed states with limited governance.

Questions & Answers

Assessment overview

In this section of the book, questions for each of the two optional content areas are given for the Paper 2 Section C A-level examination. The style of questions used in the exam has been replicated. There are some short-answer questions and some extended-writing questions. On the A-level exam papers most of the questions you will encounter are extended-writing or essay questions.

Questions worth 6 or more marks require you to:

- make connections between different parts of the subject content
- provide detailed explanations
- use examples and case studies to add geographical place detail
- back up your explanations with evidence.

It is worth thinking about the meaning of the command words you will encounter at A-level. These are shown below by increasing level of demand. Higher demand command words require higher-level thinking skills that include the ability to evaluate, draw conclusions and make judgements that are supported by evidence and make logical sense.

	Command word	Meaning	Marks
Increasing demand	Draw/plot/ complete / calculate	Add information to correctly finish a graph, map, diagram or statistical test.	1–4 marks
	Suggest	For an unfamiliar scenario, write a reasoned explanation of how or why something may occur. A suggested explanation requires justification/exemplification of a point that has been identified.	3 or 4 marks
	Explain	Provide a reasoned explanation of how or why something occurs. An explanation requires understanding to be demonstrated through the justification or exemplification of points that have been identified.	3, 4, 6 or 8 marks
	Assess	Use evidence to determine the relative significance of something. Give balanced consideration to all factors and identify which are the most important.	12 marks
	Evaluate	Measure the value or success of something and ultimately provide a balanced and substantiated judgement/conclusion. Review information and then bring it together to form a conclusion, drawing on evidence such as strengths, weaknesses, alternatives and relevant data.	20 marks

The structure of A-level Paper 2 is shown on the next page, including the questions covered by this Student Guide and those questions which are covered in accompanying Student Guides.

Paper 2 (Human geography)

Paper 2, which lasts 2 hours and 15 minutes, is marked out of 105 marks, equivalent to 30% of the A-level qualification. The breakdown of the questions is shown in the table below.

Section of Paper 2	Total marks	Typical question sequence
Section A: Globalisation and superpowers	32 marks (16 marks each)	4 and 12 marks
Section B: Shaping places (either Regenerating places OR Diverse places)	35 marks	3, 6, 6 and 20 marks
Section C: Global development and connections (either Health, human rights and intervention OR Migration, identity and sovereignty)	38 marks	4, 6, 8 and 20 marks

The sections that follow are each structured as follows:

- sample questions in the style of the examination
- levels-based mark schemes for extended questions (6 marks and over) in the style of the examination
- one student answer per question at the upper level of performance
- examiner's commentary on each of the above

Study the descriptions given after each question carefully to understand the requirements needed to achieve a high mark. You should also read the commentary with the mark schemes to understand where credit has or has not been given. In all cases, actual marks are indicated.

■ Questions

A selection of questions that are representative of the ones you will encounter in A-level Paper 2 are given in this section.

Health, human rights and intervention

Question 1

(a) Explain one reason why life expectancy varies within countries.   (4 marks)

ⓔ This question is point-marked. The mark schemes are organised into 'extended points', each for 2 marks. You should try to write an answer that makes two extended points to gain all 4 marks. An extended point consists of a basic explanation (1 mark) plus a more detailed expansion of the same explanation (1 mark). However, because the question demands 'one' reason, your points all need to be linked. You cannot get 4 marks by explaining unlinked, different reasons. You should not write a list of basic reasons, either. Note that the question wants reasons why life expectancy varies *within* countries: an answer explaining why life expectancy varies *between* the UK and India, for instance, would not answer the question.

> **Student answer**
>
> In the UK average male life expectancy is 79.5 years, but because of poverty and high unemployment it is only 75 in Blackpool and as low as 65 in some parts of Glasgow. Poverty is linked to poor diet, and higher than average levels of smoking and alcohol consumption, which in turn lead to higher levels of heart disease and diabetes, reducing life expectancy. In wealthy Dorset it is 83 years, because higher incomes mean some people can supplement NHS healthcare with private healthcare, thus improving access to health services overall and making it more likely illness is identified and treated early.

ⓔ **4/4 marks awarded** This answer takes poverty as its 'one' reason and links the extended points made to this (lifestyle, diet, access to private healthcare). The focus is on one country, and data are used to support this. The data do not score marks specifically but show detailed knowledge of the UK and this makes the explanations provided more secure. Different, but linked, explanations are provided for areas with low and high life expectancy so there are two extended points.

(b) Study **Figure 1.** Suggest why some countries provide more development aid than others.

(6 marks)

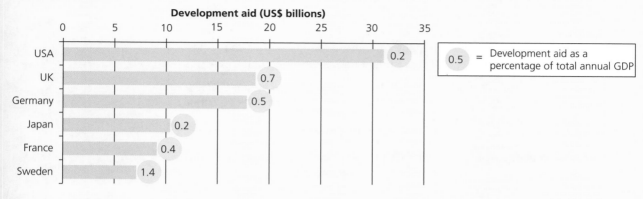

Figure 1 The top six givers of development aid in 2016

ⓔ This is a data stimulus question. Answers need to make direct reference to the information shown in Figure 1. Notice that there are two types of data shown: total development aid given by each country in US$ billions, and development aid as a percentage of GDP. Reasons should be given for variations in both. There is no need to refer to all countries for both types of data. Importantly, you should not turn these 6 mark questions into essay questions. A useful rule of thumb is to try to write three or perhaps four extended points that provide possible reasons for the information shown. Part (b) is a levels-marked question. These 6-mark 'suggest reasons' questions in A-level Paper 2 are marked using the following levels mark scheme.

Level 1	1–2 marks	■ Demonstrates isolated or generic elements of geographical knowledge and understanding, some of which may be inaccurate or irrelevant ■ Applies knowledge and understanding to geographical information inconsistently. Connections/relationships between stimulus material and the question may be irrelevant
Level 2	3–4 marks	■ Demonstrates geographical knowledge and understanding, which is mostly relevant and may include some inaccuracies ■ Applies knowledge and understanding to geographical information to find some relevant connections/relationships between stimulus material and the question
Level 3	5–6 marks	■ Demonstrates accurate and relevant geographical knowledge and understanding throughout ■ Applies knowledge and understanding to geographical information logically to find fully relevant connections/relationships between stimulus material and the question

Student answer

One reason for the variation in total amount of development aid given is simply that some of the economies are larger than others. For instance the USA's economy is ten times larger than Sweden's so the USA gives more. However, the UK gives about US$18 billion compared with Japan's US$11 billion despite UK GDP being smaller. The amount relative to GDP size is more useful data. It suggests some countries like Sweden (1.4%) and the UK (0.7%) are more generous.

This could be because human rights, and the need for development in developing countries, are more important national priorities in some countries compared with others. Countries like Japan may have a less global outlook and don't see the need to help other countries — preferring to spend their money at home. The UK and France once had many colonies, and their higher spending could be due to a sense of guilt that they should help their ex-colonies in Africa.

Lastly, Sweden and the UK have increased their aid spending to at least 0.7% of GDP because this is an agreed UN and OECD target, dating from 1970. Other countries may disagree with the target.

ⓔ **6/6 marks awarded** This is a good answer that shows clear understanding of the absolute and relative data in Figure 1, and uses both types directly in the answer. The obvious explanation related to the GDP size of the countries is outlined, plus the more subtle reasoning that the relative proportions of GDP given as aid suggest some countries prioritise helping developing countries more than others. There are also useful suggestions about relationships with ex-colonies and the global target of development aid as 0.7% of GDP. Overall, there are a range of sensible reasons given, with some depth but not so much that the answer becomes a major essay.

(c) Explain why different groups and organisations have contrasting views on the meaning of 'development'.   (8 marks)

ⓔ This question, unlike the previous 6 mark question, is not a data stimulus question. It is probably best to view these questions as 'mini essays'. They use the command word 'explain' rather than the higher demand 'assess' or 'evaluate'. This means you are providing explanations, i.e. saying why. Answers need to use examples to support explanations. These need to contain some detail, but should not be large case studies: a range of three or four brief examples will be enough. In this specific question the examples need to be of different 'groups and organisations'. Mentioning an IGO, an NGO and TNCs would be enough range. Focusing your answer on just NGOs would be very detailed, but also very narrow and would not address 'different groups and organisations'. It would be wise to pause and think about what 'development' might mean and try to break the word down: economic development, social development including human rights, greater equality — these are all interpretations of 'development'. These 8-mark 'explain' questions in A-level Paper 2 are marked using the following levels mark scheme.

Level 1	1–3 marks	▪ Demonstrates isolated elements of geographical knowledge and understanding, some of which may be inaccurate or irrelevant ▪ Understanding addresses a narrow range of geographical ideas, which lack detail
Level 2	4–6 marks	▪ Demonstrates geographical knowledge and understanding, which is mostly relevant and may include some inaccuracies ▪ Understanding addresses a range of geographical ideas, which are not fully detailed and/or developed
Level 3	7–8 marks	▪ Demonstrates accurate and relevant geographical knowledge and understanding throughout ▪ Understanding addresses a broad range of geographical ideas, which are detailed and fully developed

Student answer

Some intergovernmental organisations such as the IMF and World Trade Organization usually view development in ⓐ economic terms. This is also the view held by global TNCs such as ⓑ Nike and Walmart. To these organisations development is about increasing wealth and income through job creation and international trade. This is the 'trade is the engine of growth' model which is a ⓓ neo-liberal view of progress.

Many NGOs such as ⓑ Practical Action support a different view, that suggests development is more about meeting ⓐ basic needs of food, water and health and providing opportunities through education and greater gender equality. NGOs and others fear that focusing on economic development risks human rights abuses such as TNC worker exploitation, and creates a widening income inequality gap. Organisations like ⓑ Amnesty International specifically campaign on human rights issues which tend to discriminate against women, ⓓ indigenous groups and minority ethic groups and prevent them making development progress.

The ⓒ UN's Sustainable Development Goals for 2015–30 focus on human rights, gender equality, education and environmental issues. The ⓐ environmental focus recognises that wealth-driven development is likely to lead to urban air pollution, water pollution and other issues that negatively affect human wellbeing, health and life expectancy. Different groups and organisations are ⓔ motivated by different things such as people versus profit, or environment versus wealth, and this effects their perspective on what 'development' is.

ⓔ **8/8 marks awarded** This is a well-organised answer that shows good understanding of development. It considers development from different standpoints, namely as an ⓐ economic process, a social process and one that has to have an environmental aspect. Rather than mentioning groups and organisations only in very general terms it uses ⓑ specific examples to illustrate the explanations made — but without turning the answer into one dominated by descriptive case studies. The answer has some good up-to-date detail, such as reference to the ⓒ UN SDGs. The use of terminology, such as ⓓ 'neo-liberal' and 'indigenous groups' is very good and this demonstrates command of the subject matter. The very last ⓔ sentence is a good summary, as it refers to what motivates different groups and organisations as being key to understanding their perspective. These 8-mark 'explain' questions do not need a conclusion, but finding a focused last sentence rounds the answer off nicely.

(d) Evaluate the view that military interventions rarely improve the human rights and development situation in the countries affected.   (20 marks)

ⓔ Question (d) is an essay question. As such, detailed place knowledge and understanding in the form of examples and case studies is important. A very good answer cannot be written in only general terms. Answers need to show understanding of a range of issues and places. Often the command word 'evaluate' is used as part of the phrase 'evaluate the view'. This sets up the idea that there is more than one view to be considered, i.e. the one stated in the question plus the opposite view, or more than one alterative view. Good answers must consider more than one view, in other words provide both (or multiple) sides of the argument. Just agreeing with the view stated and not providing an alternative risks gaining around 10 marks out of 20, because only one side has been considered. The key to a high mark is understanding that 'evaluate' requires supported judgements to be made. The evidence you use (examples, data, places, facts, theories) should support your overall judgement. This needs to be confident: try to avoid sitting on the fence. There is no 'right' answer but you must provide a well-argued answer. In this specific question an answer needs to consider whether in some cases military interventions have actually worked, as well as examining situations where they have not. Good answers will make conclusions based on different examples of interventions and their outcomes. These 20-mark 'evaluate' questions in A-level Paper 2 are marked using the following levels mark scheme.

Level 1	1–5 marks	■ Demonstrates isolated elements of geographical knowledge and understanding, some of which may be inaccurate or irrelevant ■ Applies knowledge and understanding of geographical ideas, making limited and rarely logical connections/relationships ■ Applies knowledge and understanding of geographical information/ideas to produce an interpretation with limited coherence and support from evidence ■ Applies knowledge and understanding of geographical information/ideas to produce an unsupported or generic conclusion, drawn from an argument that is unbalanced or lacks coherence
Level 2	6–10 marks	■ Demonstrates geographical knowledge and understanding, which is occasionally relevant and may include some inaccuracies ■ Applies knowledge and understanding of geographical information/ideas with limited but logical connections/relationships ■ Applies knowledge and understanding of geographical ideas in order to produce a partial interpretation that is supported by some evidence but has limited coherence ■ Applies knowledge and understanding of geographical information/ideas to come to a conclusion, partially supported by an unbalanced argument with limited coherence
Level 3	11–15 marks	■ Demonstrates geographical knowledge and understanding, which is mostly relevant and accurate ■ Applies knowledge and understanding of geographical information/ideas to find some logical and relevant connections/relationships ■ Applies knowledge and understanding of geographical ideas in order to produce a partial but coherent interpretation that is supported by some evidence ■ Applies knowledge and understanding of geographical information/ideas to come to a conclusion, largely supported by an argument that may be unbalanced or partially coherent
Level 4	16–20 marks	■ Demonstrates accurate and relevant geographical knowledge and understanding throughout ■ Applies knowledge and understanding of geographical information/ideas to find fully logical and relevant connections/relationships ■ Applies knowledge and understanding of geographical information/ideas to produce a full and coherent interpretation that is supported by evidence ■ Applies knowledge and understanding of geographical information/ideas to come to a rational, substantiated conclusion, fully supported by a balanced argument that is drawn together coherently

Student answer

Military interventions [a] usually take place as a last resort when a humanitarian crisis and widespread human rights abuses are occurring. Most often this is due to civil war in a country, and a refugee crisis taking place. The United Nations [a] can deploy UN peacekeepers in these circumstances, or countries (usually Western countries) can act on their own.

The [b] 2003 invasion of Iraq by US and UK military forces was justified on the basis of human rights, as Saddam Hussein was said to be using chemical weapons on his own people, but these were never found. The invasion, and subsequent occupation until 2011, had a questionable impact on human rights and development. Iraq has struggled since to be united, the Kurdish nation in the north has split from Iraq proper and there has been constant conflict between different Islamic groups including terrorism by ISIS since 2011. Overthrowing Saddam Hussein did not lead to peace and stability, and [e] economic progress and human rights progress has been slow.

In 2007 the USA had 170,000 troops in Iraq, but even this number struggled to produce a stable political and economic situation. In [b] Libya in 2011 and during the [b] Syrian Civil War since 2012, US, French and UK governments have intervened using [c] mainly airpower rather than troops on the ground. In both cases the impact has been limited, because of the lack of direct impact on the ground. Consequently stable governments that could promote human rights have not been achieved. In addition the use of air power may destroy infrastructure on the ground that could [e] hinder recovery once conflict has ended.

However, there are examples where military intervention has been more successful. UK armed forces intervened in [d] Sierra Leone in 2000 during civil war, and after a failed UN intervention. UK involvement proved quick and decisive. French intervention in nearby [d] Côte d'Ivoire in 2010–11 had similar results: the restoration of a stable government and the resumption of development. However, [f] development aid and debt relief, not military intervention, have actually improved the situation for people in Sierra Leone and Cote d'Ivoire post-conflict. Nevertheless, military intervention helped end human rights abuses such as the use of child soldiers. The deployment of NATO forces in [d] Bosnia in 1995 has been widely viewed as successful in terms of ending the [e] genocide of Bosnian Serbs and eventually leading to the prosecution of war criminals.

Overall, military intervention can be successful in terms of ending conflict if it is targeted and relatively [g] small scale and has clear objectives. Larger interventions such as Iraq and in the 1960s and 1970s in Vietnam could be accused of simply creating more instability and therefore allowing human rights abuses to continue and development progress to reverse. Post-conflict [f] aid and reconstruction are needed to do more than just stop abuses, and create the conditions for genuine development and human rights progress.

(e) **20/20 marks awarded** This is a well structured answer with a good focus on military intervention. The answer begins with a definition and discussion (a) of military intervention. This is a good way to start, because it provides focus and shows good understanding of who carries out interventions and in what circumstances. Paragraphs two and three (b) argue the case against intervention, and there is good use of examples in terms of Iraq and Libya/Syria. There is an interesting argument (c) about whether ground forces may be more effective than the use of aircraft alone. The second half of the answer argues the alternative view that intervention can make a difference, and again real-world examples (d) are used to support this. There is also consideration of both (e) human rights and development, in a fairly balanced way. The role of (f) development aid is also considered and the answer argues that this has to be part of any long-term improvement in human rights and development — military intervention on its own is not enough. The conclusion recognises that some interventions might be (g) simpler to achieve and therefore more likely to be successful, whereas others occur in more complex circumstances and could actually make a situation worse — or simply no better.

Migration, identity and sovereignty

Question 1

(a) Explain **one** reason why the identity of products labelled as 'Made in Britain' is an increasingly complex idea.

(4 marks)

(e) This question is point-marked. The mark schemes are organised into 'extended points' each for 2 marks. You should try to write an answer that makes two extended points to gain all 4 marks. An extended point consists of a basic explanation (1 mark) plus a more detailed expansion of the same explanation (1 mark). However, because the question demands 'one' reason your points all need to be linked. You cannot get 4 marks by explaining unlinked, different reasons. You should not write a list of basic reasons, either. The focus on the question is on one small area of the specification, which is common for these short 4-mark questions: you need to make sure you know the terminology used in the specification in detail.

> **Student answer**
>
> Made in Britain is a complex idea because many products and brands that are closely linked with British national identity are now owned by foreign TNCs. This includes Jaguar Land Rover and Tetley Tea which are owned by Indian company Tata, and Rolls Royce Motors which is owned by German TNC BMW. These companies make and sell in Britain, but profits are taken back to their home country. It is also a complex idea because even British-owned companies source parts from abroad for finished goods made in Britain, and some iconic British brands like clothing retailer Burberry make their goods abroad, e.g. in China. The identity of 'Britishness' is just a perception because of globalised ownership and supply chains.

4/4 marks awarded This is a good answer which is focused on the idea of complex ownership and global production chains. The first extended point that scores 2 marks is the explanation of foreign ownership, with the use of specific examples as the extension. The idea of complexity is extended in the second explanation about how British companies use parts made abroad, and British brands are made abroad to be sold in the UK. The final sentence shows good understanding of 'identity' linked to globalisation.

(b) Study **Figure 2**. Suggest reasons for the trends in United Nations Peacekeeping force numbers between 1997 and 2016. (6 marks)

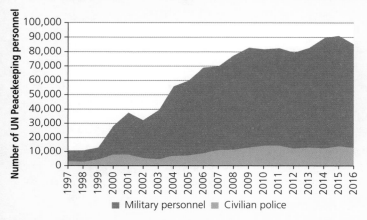

Figure 2 United Nations Peacekeeping force numbers 1997–2016

 This is a data stimulus question. Answers need to make direct reference to the information shown in Figure 2. The graph is a stacked area graph. Notice that there are two types of data shown: military personnel and civilian police. Reasons should be given for variations in both. There is a clear overall trend of increasing numbers, but also some variations from this trend. Towards the end of the time period shown the numbers stabilise somewhat. You should not turn these 6-mark questions into essay questions. A useful rule of thumb is to try to write three or perhaps four extended points that provide possible reasons for the information shown. Part (b) is a levels marked question. These 6-mark 'suggest reasons' questions in A-level Paper 2 are marked using the following levels mark scheme.

Level 1	1–2 marks	■ Demonstrates isolated or generic elements of geographical knowledge and understanding, some of which may be inaccurate or irrelevant ■ Applies knowledge and understanding to geographical information inconsistently. Connections/relationships between stimulus material and the question may be irrelevant
Level 2	3–4 marks	■ Demonstrates geographical knowledge and understanding, which is mostly relevant and may include some inaccuracies ■ Applies knowledge and understanding to geographical information to find some relevant connections/relationships between stimulus material and the question
Level 3	5–6 marks	■ Demonstrates accurate and relevant geographical knowledge and understanding throughout ■ Applies knowledge and understanding to geographical information logically to find fully relevant connections/relationships between stimulus material and the question

Student answer

The overall trend is a very large increase in UN peacekeepers from 10,000 in 1997 to 80,000–90,000 in the period 2013–16. This increase could be because the UN and UN member states are more willing to get involved in conflicts such as Syria or the DRC, or that there have been more conflicts recently than in the late 1990s.

The fact that most of the increase is accounted for by military personnel, rather than civilian police, suggests any increase in the number of conflicts are armed warfare rather than less serious situations. Since 2009 overall numbers have been fairly stable which could suggest either fewer new conflicts or that existing conflicts are continuing and long-running. The dip in numbers in 2001–02 from 37,000 to 32,000 could mark the successful end of a conflict and its peacekeeping mission.

Lastly, the data are only for UN peacekeepers so may not reflect the extent of conflict worldwide as in conflicts such as Syria there are US, Russian and Turkish troops involved but few UN forces.

ⓔ **6/6 marks awarded** This is a well-organised answer. It breaks Figure 2 down into sections and provides possible reasons for the different trends identified. This is a good way to approach the data you are asked to look at, because it provides a natural structure for your answer. The answer mentions both military personnel and civilian police, and uses data from the y-axis of the graph: this adds accuracy. The reasons provided are all realistic. As you would not have seen these data before, your reasons need to be sensible but there is some room for speculation — such as the idea that recently the number of conflicts has stabilised, or that UN Peacekeeping forces are not used in some conflicts. This answer provides a range of extended reasons without turning the question into a long essay, which would risk running out of time later on in the question paper and should be avoided.

(c) **Explain why intergovernmental organisations (IGOs) have been formed to attempt to manage some environmental problems.** (8 marks)

ⓔ This question, unlike the previous 6-mark question, is not a data stimulus question. It is probably best to view these questions as 'mini essays'. They use the command word 'explain' rather than the higher demand 'assess' or 'evaluate'. This means you are providing explanations, i.e. saying why. Answers need to use examples to support explanations. These must contain some detail, but should not be large case studies: a range of three or four brief examples will be enough. One of the important points to consider about this specific question is that both 'IGOs' and 'environmental problems' are plural. This means an answer that only focuses on one IGO and one problem will lack the range needed to score more than low Level 2 marks. In addition, the question isn't focused on what the IGOs do as much as why they were formed: why does the world need IGOs/global action on environmental problems? Be careful not to focus on long descriptions of the actions of IGOs. Instead, explain their role and importance. These 8-mark 'explain' questions in A-level Paper 2 are marked using the following levels mark scheme.

Level 1	1–3 marks	▪ Demonstrates isolated elements of geographical knowledge and understanding, some of which may be inaccurate or irrelevant ▪ Understanding addresses a narrow range of geographical ideas, which lack detail
Level 2	4–6 marks	▪ Demonstrates geographical knowledge and understanding, which is mostly relevant and may include some inaccuracies ▪ Understanding addresses a range of geographical ideas, which are not fully detailed and/or developed
Level 3	7–8 marks	▪ Demonstrates accurate and relevant geographical knowledge and understanding throughout ▪ Understanding addresses a broad range of geographical ideas, which are detailed and fully developed

Student answer

IGOs are organisations that work across international borders and allow c sovereign states to cooperate on global issues. By their very nature, many environmental issues are global in scale and their impacts do not recognise political borders. The d 1987 a Montreal Protocol was organised by the UN to respond to the threat of ozone depletion by CFCs. It was formed and agreed rapidly because the threat was b serious and immediate according to scientists, and action needed to be taken. Action by individual developed countries would not have had the same impact.

The Convention on International Trade in Endangered Species a (CITES) was needed because of the specific threat of elephant ivory, rare birds and animal skins being b traded across international borders. In force since d 1975, 183 sovereign states have signed up to it, allowing for effective policing of illegal trade. Without CITES, dozens of national laws would be the only way to stop illegal trade and this would be unworkable.

UNCLOS a is the part of the UN that manages oceans in terms of sovereign rights over c exclusive economic zones and how international waters are used. UNCLOS is needed because without it the oceans could be a b 'free for all' as they are an example of 'global commons' not owned by sovereign states. UNCLOS regulates pollution and use of ocean resources. In summary, e IGOs are formed because many environmental issues can only be managed at a global level, so supranational laws and regulations are needed.

e 8/8 marks awarded This is a well-written answer that strikes the right balance between breadth and depth. The specification contains around six IGOs/treaties that could be mentioned, but trying to cover all of them would tend to produce a list rather than an explanation. Three examples a are explained here, with some detail for each. There are a range of reasons b provided for why IGOs are set up, including regulating cross-border trade, urgency of action and regulating global commons. Each reason is linked to a specific named example. The use of terminology c such as 'sovereign states' rather than the more general 'countries' shows good understanding of the subject matter. The inclusion of d dates and details shows that understanding has some depth behind it. The e final sentence is a useful summary: an evaluative conclusion is not needed for 'explain' questions but a summative sentence is useful.

(d) Evaluate the view that international migration has more costs than benefits.   (20 marks)

ⓔ Question (d) is an essay question. As such, detailed place knowledge and understanding in the form of examples and case studies is important. A very good answer cannot be written in only general terms. Answers need to show understanding of a range of issues and places. Often the command word 'evaluate' is used as part of the phrase 'evaluate the view'. This sets up the idea that there is more than one view to be considered, i.e. the one stated in the question plus the opposite view, or more than one alterative view. Good answers must consider more than one view, in other words provide both (or multiple) sides of the argument. Just agreeing with the view stated and not providing an alternative risks gaining around 10 marks out of 20, because only one side has been considered. The key to a high mark is understanding that 'evaluate' requires supported judgements to be made. The evidence you use (examples, data, places, facts, theories) should support your overall judgement. This needs to be confident: try to avoid sitting on the fence. There is no 'right' answer but you must provide a well-argued answer. For this specific question you could fall into the trap of simply agreeing that international migration does have more costs than benefits. However, a good answer will consider situations where it has more benefits than costs. Much will depend on who holds the view, as the views of different players on the immigration issue are often contrasting. These 20-mark 'evaluate' questions in A-level Paper 2 are marked using the following levels mark scheme.

Level 1	1–5 marks	■ Demonstrates isolated elements of geographical knowledge and understanding, some of which may be inaccurate or irrelevant ■ Applies knowledge and understanding of geographical ideas, making limited and rarely logical connections/relationships ■ Applies knowledge and understanding of geographical information/ideas to produce an interpretation with limited coherence and support from evidence ■ Applies knowledge and understanding of geographical information/ideas to produce an unsupported or generic conclusion, drawn from an argument that is unbalanced or lacks coherence
Level 2	6–10 marks	■ Demonstrates geographical knowledge and understanding, which is occasionally relevant and may include some inaccuracies ■ Applies knowledge and understanding of geographical information/ideas with limited but logical connections/relationships ■ Applies knowledge and understanding of geographical ideas in order to produce a partial interpretation that is supported by some evidence but has limited coherence ■ Applies knowledge and understanding of geographical information/ideas to come to a conclusion, partially supported by an unbalanced argument with limited coherence
Level 3	11–15 marks	■ Demonstrates geographical knowledge and understanding, which is mostly relevant and accurate ■ Applies knowledge and understanding of geographical information/ideas to find some logical and relevant connections/relationships ■ Applies knowledge and understanding of geographical ideas in order to produce a partial but coherent interpretation that is supported by some evidence ■ Applies knowledge and understanding of geographical information/ideas to come to a conclusion, largely supported by an argument that may be unbalanced or partially coherent

Level 4	16–20 marks	■ Demonstrates accurate and relevant geographical knowledge and understanding throughout ■ Applies knowledge and understanding of geographical information/ideas to find fully logical and relevant connections/relationships ■ Applies knowledge and understanding of geographical information/ideas to produce a full and coherent interpretation that is supported by evidence ■ Applies knowledge and understanding of geographical information/ideas to come to a rational, substantiated conclusion, fully supported by a balanced argument that is drawn together coherently

Student answer

International migration involves the **a** movement of people across international borders, usually for work as economic migrants but sometimes as refugees seeking safety from conflict or persecution. In 2018 the global stock of international migrants was close to 250 million, up from 150 million in 1990. Globalisation and migration are **b** strongly linked, with the former process promoting the latter. International migration has become increasingly political in the last decade.

Migration has a wide range of **c** economic benefits. In many developed countries migrants provide a pool of low-cost labour. The **e** USA's farming economy relies heavily on Mexican labour (some of it illegal), as do farms in the **e** UK that employ Bulgarian and Romanian EU migrants. The **e** UAE, Kuwait and Qatar rely on South Asian workers in the construction and domestic service sectors. Migrants lower costs for businesses, fill skills gaps and their mobility makes them responsive to business demand. **d** However, migrants have been accused of 'stealing jobs' from citizens. In the UK there is little evidence for this, but there is some evidence that a large pool of migrants lowers average pay. Not all international migration is low skill. Developed countries often have very open migration policies towards high-skill graduates, entrepreneurs and business people who are viewed as having a high potential to contribute to economic growth.

Socially **c** migration can be helpful, but also problematic. As most international migrants are under 40 they can boost the population of countries experiencing ageing populations. This has occurred in the UK, with fertility rates since 2005 much higher than in the few decades before. The **e** UK NHS and care sector rely heavily on EU and post-colonial migrants to provide the labour required by social and health services. **d** However, communities can undergo rapid and in some cases unwelcome change when large numbers of migrants arrive in a short space of time, such as **e** Boston in Lincolnshire, whose population of eastern Europeans increased from almost 0% in 2000 to 15% by 2015. The erosion of local or national identity resulting from cultural change brought about by immigration can become a social and political issue.

The **c** political costs of international migration are perhaps the most significant, especially when voters perceive policy has led to unsustainable levels of immigration. In Germany, Chancellor Merkel was accused of irresponsibility in allowing 1 million refugees from Syria, Iraq and North Africa to enter **e** Germany in 2015–16. Immigration policy was a key factor in the **e** UK EU referendum in 2016 and the US presidential election in the same year. However, the issue is really one of **f** scale and pace: when a proportion of the host population perceive large numbers of immigrants are arriving, possibly illegally, too quickly the positive economic and social benefits of migration quickly become overwhelmed by negative politics.

In conclusion, international migration has broadly g positive economic impacts as it usually helps balance demand for labour with supply. In terms of social and cultural impacts, the costs and benefits are more g balanced and numbers and speed of arrival seem to be key factors. Politically there can be serious g costs, especially when immigration policy is perceived to be out of balance by a significant section of the voting public. International migration can then become a divisive political issue as seen recently in the UK, USA and Germany.

e **20/20 marks awarded** This is a good answer to a very open question, which could be difficult to answer in the circumstances of the exam. This is the type of question that says 'Where do I start?' because it is broad. This answer, sensibly, begins a with a definition of international migration and links the issue to globalisation. This b connection shows good understanding of the recent context of migration. The whole answer is structured around three main c sections dealing with economic, social/cultural and political impacts. This is a clear and logical way to organise the answer and avoids the risk of drifting away from the question. Within each main section, both d costs and benefits are considered, so overall there is a balanced argument. Good use of e examples is made, and these cover a wide range of places and migration situations so the answer has breadth. The paragraph on political impacts recognises that these are largely negative, but f explains the circumstances whereby public opinion can turn against immigration. The conclusion provides both a concise summary and a clear g judgement on the balance of cost and benefits for economic, social and political consequences.

Knowledge check answers

1 Mexico (highest) and Egypt (lowest)
2 12.2 years
3 Sub-Saharan Africa
4 Glasgow
5 Sweden and Costa Rica
6 Developing countries (MDGs) and all countries (SDGs)
7 1948
8 The European Court of Human Rights
9 War crimes and crimes against humanity
10 Full democracy
11 Myanmar nationality
12 Six years
13 15 (five permanent and ten others)
14 From Myanmar, to Bangladesh
15 Africa
16 The World Health Organization (WHO)
17 The Ogoni people
18 The USA
19 Human Development Index (HDI)
20 Africa, the Middle East
21 The USA, UK and France
22 Iraq
23 Former colonies

24 Over US$9 billion
25 About 90 million
26 3.3%
27 10 million
28 22.5%
29 States in the Southeast, Southwest and Northwest
30 South Asia (India, Pakistan, Bangladesh)
31 The people, or peoples, of a state
32 Chinese
33 2008 and 2014
34 The 1950s and 1960s
35 13.1%
36 The UK
37 The Second World War
38 The USA together with the EU
39 Iran's development of nuclear weapons
40 The Arab Spring
41 Africa
42 14 years (1973 to 1987)
43 Through teaching 'Fundamental British Values'
44 2%
45 India
46 Media, fast food and retailing
47 Spain and France
48 Environmental issues and pollution

Index

Note: **Bold** page numbers indicate defined terms.

Index